HOW TO

COOK PRAYER

HOW TO COOK PRAYER

Copyright © 2022 Victor Ansor
America Intercessory Prayer Group Inc.
A Victor Ansor Ministries
All Rights Reserved.

No rights claimed for public domain material, all rights reserved. No parts of this publication may be reproduced, stored in any retrieval system, or transmitted in any form or by any means, electronic, mechanical, recording, or otherwise, without the prior written permission of the author. Violations may be subject to civil or criminal penalties.

Library of Congress Control Number:

ISBN: 978-1-7349631-5-1 (paperback)
ISBN: 978-1-7349631-6-8 (eBook)
ISBN: 978-1-7349631-2-0 (Hardback)

Cover Design by Victor Ansor

VICTOR ANSOR PUBLISHING INC

22901 Linden Blvd
PO Box 110423
Cambria Heights NY 11411

Email: victoransor@yahoo.com
website: victoransor.com

All scriptures used are quoted in their respective translations and referred. All sources duly cited.

Printed in the United States of America

A COMPREHENSIVE GLOBAL PRAYER MANUAL
FOR EFFECTIVE CHRISTIAN LIVING

HOW TO COOK PRAYER

How to Cook Prayer with Recipes That Move Heaven And Bring a Speedy Answer

VICTOR ANSOR

VICTOR ANSOR PUBLISHING INC

Also, by the Author

The Spirit of Servanthood

How to Be Ten Times
Better than Your Peers

War in The Heavens

Global Holocaust

A Letter to My Late Mom

Why You Should ~~Not~~ Pay Your Tithe

TABLE OF CONTENTS

THIS BOOK IS DEDICATED xi

THE MANDATE xiii

ACKNOWLEDGMENT xv

APPRECIATION xvii

ANCHOR SCRIPTURE xix

INTRODUCTION 21

CHAPTER 1: WHAT IS PRAYER? 27

CHAPTER 2: THE POWER OF PRAYER 35

CHAPTER 3: WHY WE NEED TO PRAY 57

CHAPTER 4: WHEN TO PRAY 73

CHAPTER 5: WHERE TO PRAY 87

CHAPTER 6: PRAYER DURATION 91

CHAPTER 7: HOW TO PRAY 97

CHAPTER 8: TYPES OF PRAYER 117

CHAPTER 9: PRAYER CODE 175

CHAPTER 10: WHAT MAKES PRAYER EFFECTIVE 179

CHAPTER 11: HEART CONNECTIVITY 185

CHAPTER 12: PRAYER PATTERN 191

CHAPTER 13: PRAYER POSTURE 199

CHAPTER 14: THE MERCY SEAT 203

CHAPTER 15: THE COURT OF HEAVEN 209

CHAPTER 16: PERSONAL ALTAR 215

CHAPTER 17: FAMILY ALTAR 221

CHAPTER 18: PRIESTHOOD 227

CHAPTER 19: THE POWER OF INTERCESSION 237

CHAPTER 20: IMPORTUNITY IN PRAYER 247

CHAPTER 21: PRAYING TO RECEIVE ANSWER 253

CHAPTER 22: COOKING TIME OF PRAYER 261

CHAPTER 23: PRAYER SPICES 265

CHAPTER 24: STEAM OF FAITH 275

CHAPTER 25: THE SALT OF PURITY 279

CHAPTER 26: INGREDIENT OF RIGHTEOUSNESS 287

CHAPTER 27: ADDING FASTING TO PRAYER 293

CHAPTER 28: THE COOKING POT OF PRAYER 309

CHAPTER 29: AVOID DOUBT 315

CHAPTER 30: NIGHT PRAYER 321

CHAPTER 31: WRESTLING WITH YOUR ANGEL 337

CHAPTER 32: THE SPIRIT OF GRACE AND SUPPLICATION 345

EPILOGUE 351

THIS BOOK IS DEDICATED

*To the prayer warriors and intercessors who
keeps the fire on the prayer altar burning,
cooking the prayer that advances
the purposes of God on the earth.*

The Mandate

Unto me, who am less than the least of all saints, is this grace given, that I should preach among the Gentiles the unsearchable riches of Christ; And to make all men see what is the fellowship of the mystery, which from the beginning of the world had been hid in God, who created all things by Jesus Christ: To the intent that now unto the principalities and powers in heavenly places might be known by the church the manifold wisdom of God, According to the eternal purpose which he purposed in Christ Jesus our Lord

Ephesians 3:8-11

Acknowledgment

I acknowledge the almighty God, my Father in heaven, for granting me life. Without Him, I could do nothing. I also acknowledge the person of the Holy Spirit who is my faithful companion. Wisdom and understanding I have none and without the help of the Holy Spirit, I would not be able to write this or any other book. I always sit back to read what I have written and every time I wonder how I did it. To me, that means I am not the one who wrote it, instead, it was the Holy Spirit who wrote through me.

This book and all my books have impacted my life and I hope they impact the lives of my readers. By the grace of God, I am just a pen of a ready writer, and I count it a great privilege to be in the service of

God and to be an instrument He uses to propagate His Word.

I am thankful to my mother Mrs. Agatha, who has gone to be with the Lord. May her soul continue to rest in the Lord until we meet again when the trumpet sounds. She was instrumental to my being in Christ today. She taught me how to pray.

Finally, I want to thank you, my readers. Without you, there would be no book. I also want to thank everyone who has encouraged me in one way or the other. May God bless you abundantly.

Appreciation

I want to thank all my readers and those who encourage me to keep writing. I want to thank you all for your support and words of encouragement. I want to thank all my friends and those who were instrumental to the successful completion of this book.

Finally, I want to thank those who are unwavering in their prayer adventure for my life and ministry. You are the reason why I am still standing today. May you be greatly rewarded. God bless you.

For Agatha

Anchor Scripture

Philippians 4:6

Be careful for nothing; but in every thing by prayer and supplication with thanksgiving let your requests be made known unto God. KJV

Introduction

Everybody prays.

Prayer is one thing that everyone involves in irrespective of race, language, or religion. Prayer is made day and night all over the world every minute of the day to a deity. Although everybody prays yet not everyone prays to Jehovah the God of our Lord Jesus. Not everyone knows how to pray, nor what is involved in making prayer worthwhile. **Prayer is a deliberate act and not a spontaneous engagement as many supposed**. The reason why some Christians do not pray and why prayer meetings are always dry with few people is because of the lack of interest. Prayer, like food, has a recipe and the knowledge of the prayer recipe is what brings outstanding results and engagement interesting.

HOW TO COOK PRAYER

To pray effectively, one must be taught. Like food preparation, you must learn it from somewhere. You were either taught to cook by your parents, family member, or a friend. By all means, you must have learned somewhere how to cook. If you have never learned how to cook and you go to the market to pick some items and start cooking, we are sure that food will not be eaten by you or anyone else. Prayer is like cooking food, as explained above, not all turns out right or tastes the same. In the school of prayer, everyone is a student, you cannot graduate from prayer unless you are no longer in existence. There is no professor emeritus in the school of prayer, everyone is a perpetual student. If you are not taught how to pray, you may remain in the elementary shouting and screaming level where you will only get reluctant, frustrated, and quit praying.

Then we may ask, how do we pray, and how should we prepare our prayer? These and other questions have answers in this book as we look at the subject of prayer from the perspective of a chef.

Although everybody prays, not everyone prays to God, and not every prayer receives an answer. Prayer has a pattern, protocol, and method that when engaged will produce an outstanding result. There is a way to make prayer; prayer must be cooked following a meticulous method. Remember that when you want to cook or when a chef wants to cook a meal, there are procedures to follow to make the cooking a success. There is what you begin with and when to add certain ingredients and the time for steaming. A mistake or error in adding or steaming can ruin what could have been a delicious meal.

Salt, although very important in the cooking process, could cause great disaster if not added in the required quantity. So is prayer; if you don't follow the process and know what to pray or add at the appropriate time, can result in wasted effort. Prayer is like preparing a meal, you do not wake up and jump to the kitchen and start cooking. A lot of things are involved in cooking and so is prayer. Before a meal is prepared, a lot of mental activities go into it.

HOW TO COOK PRAYER

In fact, switching on the stove to cook is the final process in the art of cooking.

Days before my mother cooks, she will either buy on her way from work or send me or my siblings to pick up some groceries in the market. The food is days away, but my mother already figured out what is required to make the anticipated meal. She lists out things that she needs that are not available at home and makes sure everybody is involved in getting them ready. When these items are in place, a night prior she would ask us to get certain things out of the freezer so that they can defrost before daybreak. On the D-day, she takes time to prepare the food items before she puts the pot on the fire. You see, cooking is not an emergency thing, especially if you want to have a quality meal.

Prayer like food has a process. You don't jump into prayer or else you will come out empty. You must know what you want to pray about, and the things involved to make that prayer turn out right. Before you knock on heaven's gate, gather the prayer items, put a lot of mental preparation to cook a delicious prayer meal and you will come out sweating and licking the plate.

I therefore invite you to put on your apron and join me as we enter the prayer kitchen to cook answers delivering prayer.

Chapter 1

What Is Prayer?

Jeremiah 29:12
Then shall ye call upon me, and ye shall go and pray unto me, and I will hearken unto you. KJV

Prayer is a channel through which man interacts with God. Prayer is an earthly communication line that allows man to reach his maker at any point in time. Through prayer, human beings can have access to the creator who lives trillions of light-years away. It is the fastest way to call for help from a realm that is far from ours. God is the creator of the universe, and he lives in heaven. Man, the created being cannot see God nor have access to Him. It is in the place of prayer that man can see, hear, and interact with his creator. Prayer is an access route. It is a prayer that reveals that God is nearer to earth and man than we think.

Mark 6:46

And when he had sent them away,
he departed into a mountain to pray. KJV

When Jesus was here on earth, it is recorded that he often goes up the mountain to pray. Jesus understood that he could do nothing without interacting with God. Without prayer, Jesus would not have accomplished his mission. Jesus the son of the living God depended so much on prayer to fulfill his mission. I thought that since he was the son of God, he did not necessarily need to pray because God is his father. Remember, Jesus came from heaven to earth, he was one hundred percent human and one hundred percent God. But he needed help from the realm where he came from to succeed in the mission he was sent to do.

If the son of God needed prayer to succeed, then we have no choice but to pray. Prayer is therefore that part of our lives we cannot do away with or do without. It is not something we do once at a time or when we like.

Prayer is as much of an essence to life as eating and drinking. Without prayer, we cannot survive on this earth. A prayerless person is a rag that the devil uses to rub his legs whenever he comes out of the mud. You cannot live a fulfilled and fruitful Christian life without giving yourself to prayer. It is a prayer that summons God who is a spirit into our affairs. Prayer is that important because, without it, God has no business on earth. **It is a prayer that summons spirits.** We started by saying that everybody prays but not everyone summons God. The spirit realm depends on prayer and who you pray to determines what happens in your life, family, and environment. When God created this world, he gave man dominion over the affairs of the earth.

HOW TO COOK PRAYER

Genesis 1:26

And God said, Let us make man in our image, after our likeness: and let them have dominion over the fish of the sea, and over the fowl of the air, and over the cattle, and over all the earth, and over every creeping thing that creepeth upon the earth. KJV

The man was given dominion over the earth which means that God cannot operate on the earth without the permission of man according to the scripture above. Does God have the power? Yes, but if He overrides the authority he gave to man, then He will not be true to His word, and we would not call Him faithful or trust Him. This is the reason why He (God) couldn't keep our first parent from eating the fruit. Not to digress; before God does anything on the earth, He needs a man to carry it out. When He needed to redeem man, He came through His son Jesus by giving him a body to operate on the earth.

VICTOR ANSOR

Hebrew 10:5

Wherefore when he cometh into the world, he saith, Sacrifice and offering thou wouldest not, but a body hast thou prepared me. KJV

This makes man so important in the universal scheme of things. The devil and his demons depend on the body of man to operate effectively on the earth. This is why there are so many atrocities committed by man and you wonder how a human being could be so cruel. The devil uses the body of man through his demons to express himself and his desire daily. For demons to operate in any region or locality, they need the body of a man, Mark 5:9.

Spirits are not permitted to operate on the earth including God but through the human body, they can have access. This is the reason why there is madness on the increase everywhere around the world. Remember the lunatic man of Gadarenes in Luke 8:30, he had a legion of demons' resident in him. They refused to leave the territory but begged to stay. This is what we call familiar spirits. The spirits of ancestors that controls a region or community could be resident in one man, animal, or tree, and whenever something removes them from their abode, they look for another house to stay. Prayer, therefore, is the platform that man can use to interact with God to function on the earth.

Understand that no man on this earth is without the help of a spirit. If you must accomplish anything important in this life, a spirit must give you a helping hand. You may say that you never ask for help from any spirit, you could be right. But wait until you make the kind of money that no one in your lineage ever made or reach a position of authority then they will come for you. The spirit you never interacted with will certainly come for you. Sometimes a spirit can help you succeed only to appear later to demand your soul. God, who is a Spirit, can help you to succeed, and later He comes for you. Before you realize, you become a born-again Christian and begin to use the resources you thought were yours to advance His purposes. That is the way of the spirit, and that is the way this realm is structured. You need prayer to live, and prayer brings a spirit into your affairs. King David said something very profound in Psalm 144:1

Blessed be the Lord my strength which teacheth my hands to war, and my fingers to fight. KJV

David a man said that God who is a spirit taught him how to fight. From the scriptures, we know that king David was a man of prayer and his interaction with the God of heaven brought him into such a dimension of exploits in life. He said that a spirit taught him how to fight battles.

Prayer is the only means through which we seek help from God who is a Spirit. Without prayer life would be difficult and things may not work for us as we intended. It is important for us to live a prayerful life as this is the only way through which we interact with the heavenly realm.

Prayer is a means of communicating with God. If we don't pray, then we cannot have access to God. The only way a man can reach God is through prayer, Jeremiah 29:12. God expects us to call on Him in prayer. If we don't pray, then we starve ourselves of fellowship with God. If one stays without praying to God, such a person will be open to many afflictions of life. Prayer is what connects us to God and brings His blessing and protection. As you keep the channel of prayer open, God will take charge of your life and keep you from evil in Jesus' name.

Chapter 2

The Power of Prayer

2 Corinthians 10:4

For the weapons of our warfare are not carnal, but mighty through God to the pulling down of strong holds; KJV

Prayer is a powerful weapon that can pull down strongholds. Demonic strongholds are not seen with the naked eye neither can you fight them nor breakthrough with a physical weapon or strength. The entire global arsenal cannot pull down a demonic stronghold. Prayer is the only weapon that when you engage, everything gives way. **When you pray, anything can happen**. The forces of darkness do not want a believer to pray and so they throw all sorts of arrows just to keep us from prayer.

As a born-again Christian, the only way you can succeed is by prayer. The enemy does not want you to advance in life or exceed the quota they set for your family. Yes, every family has a limit that the demonic world has placed them, and the only way you can break through that limitation is through prayer.

We do not know the power of prayer until we engage effectively. If you are a prayerful Christian, you become a person of interest in your territory. The witches and warlocks know you and will try everything to stop you. They can only succeed if you stop praying. If you notice that you are losing interest in prayer or that anytime you want to pray, you become sleepy, know that it is an attack, and call for backup. You can partner with someone to make sure you continue praying or play gospel songs that can motivate you to pray. Any attack from the enemy on your prayer life should not scare you but make you know that you are doing something that is affecting the kingdom of darkness.

Be aware that the demonic world knows you, your bank information, health condition, children, business, and everything concerning you. As soon as you break through a certain limit in business, career, family life, or finance, they will check your family's limit and launch an attack. I don't mean to scare you but to put you on your feet to pray because there is power in prayer.

It is important to know that prayer when engaged, destroys the camp of the enemy. That is why as a child of God, you can be full of activities without getting tired but as soon as you decide to pray, all hell breaks loose. You can watch all the series on the TV for hours without a blink of an eye, but the moment you start praying if care is not taken, you will see yourself five hours later sleeping on your knees. Don't think that it is normal or that you were tired. If you were on social media or your friend was on the phone with you at the same time, you would not have slept.

The enemy fights our prayer lives so we can be weak spiritually. Anyone who is suffering from insomnia or has difficulty sleeping should be prescribed prayer pills and that sickness will vanish without a trace. Ask the person to kneel and pray and you will be surprised how quickly they will sleep.

The devil does not want anyone to pray to God. If you are praying to God, the devil will do anything to stop you. Prayer is a very powerful weapon, and the devil is afraid of it. That is why demonic forces will do anything to keep people from engaging in prayer. The only way you can fight your enemy is through prayer. If you are confronted with any issue or challenge, all you need to do is pray. When you pray, the arsenal of heaven is discharged at your disposal. The angels of God are waiting for your prayer and immediately after you start praying, they go to work. If you are a born-again Christian and prayerless, your angels will be very lazy and fat because you have not given them any job.

Prayer provokes the power of God on our behalf and sends the devil packing out of our lives. Some born-again Christians have demonic forces open a kiosk in their home, office, family, or business. But at the instance of prayer, the devil's business will be closed, he will file for bankruptcy, and demons will run seeking where to hide.

The Bible says that the weapons of our warfare are not earthly but spiritual and they can pull down the stronghold of darkness. Have you ever seen a demonic stronghold before? I believe not, but your prayer can see it and pull it down. The force of prayer can discover demonic attachments or deposits in your life and dissolve them. The only way you can fight demons and evil spirits are through prayer. The power of prayer is stronger and mightier than the entire United States military and its allies. Never underestimate what prayer can do. The more you pray, the more victory you have, the less you pray, the weaker you become spiritually; I have experienced both.

HOW TO COOK PRAYER

The difference between a victorious Christian and a victim is prayer. Prayer keeps the enemy away from our lives and procures blessings and breakthroughs. Let me tell you, no matter the amount of blessing a man of God releases upon you, if you are prayerless it will not work. God can honor the prayer of the pastor because of his standing with Him and release mercy drops which many think is a blessing but to receive from God, you must pray. I was prayerless at a time in my life and I know how I suffered. I stagnated for a long time, and nothing was working. I experienced setbacks, disappointments, near-success syndrome, and much misfortune until I gave myself to prayer and things turned around and began to work for me.

When you know the power of prayer, you will be excited to pray. I became so addicted to prayer that my roommates once asked me why I prayed so much. When my breakthrough came, they said they now understand. Everybody uses something. No one advances in life with a clear eye. You cannot compete for a contract and pray five minutes in the morning and go to contend with people who cooked themselves the night before. Not everybody sleeps at night. While you are snoring at night, your contender is mingling with spirits, and when he or she gets the job or contract you ask God why.

Prayer is a powerful weapon and the only weapon that you need to win the battle of life. This world we are living in is very deep and if you do not pray, you will become a welcome doormat that everyone marches on. The arrow the enemy is throwing at you and your family can only be returned through prayer.

Be aware that as soon as you give your life to Jesus, you become a person of interest in the demonic world. A price will be put on your head to bring you down and finally destroyed. What will make them not succeed is prayer. If you want to know if your environment is cleared of evil or not, engage in prayer and you will be surprised. Prayer can reveal what the naked eye cannot see. Prayer can show you what has been done against your child not doing well in school. It can show you why your husband or wife starts misbehaving or why you suddenly lost that job or contract. Prayer is a revelator of secrets and if you have any doubt about an issue in your life or want to know the why's in your life, engage in prayer.

A prayer weapon never fails and is very potent. The opening scripture says that the weapon of our warfare is not earthly but mighty, this means that prayer is so powerful beyond earthly understanding. With prayer, we can move mountains and create a path that did not exist. With prayer, we can reroute the arrows of the wicked and send them back to the sender. With prayer, we can undo every wicked plan of the enemy and silence the evil tongue of judgment.

Before I got married, I thought that life was good as I was enjoying the blessing of God, and everywhere was quiet. I was having fun and enjoying the ride of life until I proposed to my wife and all hell broke loose. I was prompted to engage in a series of prayers before my wedding and things began to happen. People that I thought were relatives and friends suddenly turned against me and my wife, it came from both sides. The apartment where I lived and never had any problem threatened to take me to court if I continue to pray the way I was praying. I got strange knocks on my door at midnight and mysterious notes were placed on my door threatening me. My wife's auntie threatened to stop the marriage and discourage everyone she knew from associating with us. Many weird things happened just because I engaged in prayer. You see, prayer can discover things.

When you don't pray, nothing will happen, and you will think life is good until you give yourself to prayer and be amazed at what will happen. If you suspect somebody of anything, the only way to know is to engage in prayer. Prayer can get you a wife or husband. Prayer can reveal to you why you are barren or impotent. Prayer can show you who is planning your downfall and the source of that sickness, disease, or delay in breakthrough.

Know that there is no powerful man of God but a prayerful man of God. It is prayer that distinguishes pastors from pastors. Those you think are great men of God with power have nothing else than a prayerful life. God will not move in your life as He supposed until you give yourself to prayer. It is a prayer that helps us to fulfill our purpose in life. Prayer is so powerful that the devil and his agents are afraid when you pray. Your angel will bring you so many blessings if you are prayerful.

There are many hanging blessings in the spirit realm and many confiscated blessings. Only prayer can release them. I used to see my cars in the dream until I prayed and the same colors I used to see, are the same I am driving now. There was a time I use to see myself in school sitting in a lecture room until I prayed and now, I have a master's degree and I don't have such a dream anymore. Some things you see in the dream are your blessings trapped in the spirit world and if you don't pray, you will never have them. It is time you stop running around looking for pastors to pray for you but rather cook yourself in prayer and things will turn around in such a way that you will think it's a dream.

Many Christians don't know the power of prayer which is why they don't pray. Many think that the corporate prayer in church is enough not knowing that without a personal prayer life, they will not advance. You must learn how to harness the power of God in your life by cooking yourself on the prayer altar.

In Africa where I come from, people go to the juju priest, and they prepare a potion for them. This potion is then put in a big pot with water and the priest will carry the man and put him inside the pot and cook. When this is done, the man will come out very powerful, he can disappear at will and no knife or bullet can penetrate him.

Do you know you can operate in a higher dimension than that man if you cook yourself on the prayer altar? Prayer is more powerful than the juju priest cooking pot. Don't live your life as if the world is a very nice and harmless place. You need the power to operate in this world and prayer is the only way you can harness the power needed to live. This world is very wicked, the bible says in the book of Psalm 74:20

> *Have respect unto the covenant: for the dark places of the earth are full of the habitations of cruelty.* KJV

There is so much wickedness in this world that if you don't cook yourself in prayer, those who cook themselves in dark places will use you as football kicking you about as they like. If you think that your children in school are safe, think again because you don't know who their teachers are. Why do you think a child that was very smart suddenly become a dullard? Or as soon as a husband got the promotion he has been waiting for, he starts seeing another woman? Many situations that we think are normal may be manipulated from a different realm and the only way to stay aloft is through prayer.

One day while growing up, I came back from school, and a hand slapped me on my head in the house from nowhere. I did not see the hand, but I felt it. If not for my mother's prayer I would not have survived. The plan was to stop me from succeeding academically but to the glory of God, I have all the degrees I wanted and more to come because somebody cooked me in prayer.

Prayer is very powerful and if you want to keep your family safe, cook them in prayer. As a wife, you can cook your husband and children in prayer. As a husband, keep your family secure on the prayer altar and the evil forces of darkness will be far from them. Do not take any step without first cooking yourself on the prayer altar and when you come out, you will be too hot for the devil to handle. Stop trusting people and relax thinking they are harmless, fortify yourself and everything that concerns you. Whether they are white, black, or brown, everybody uses something, and you too use something and when you appear, other powers will submit. The Bible says in Psalm 66:3

> *Say unto God, How terrible art thou in thy works! through the greatness of thy power shall thine enemies submit themselves unto thee.* KJV

The devil and his agents will only submit if you are powerful, and prayer is the only way to secure power. Pray days before you go for any exam or interview, and you will be successful. I did not know this, and I went on a series of interviews and failed. Something very insignificant would cause me to fail the interview and I wondered why.

The reason why you are blaming a witch for your misfortune is that you don't give yourself to prayer. When you pray, no witch will be able to stand before you. In America and Europe, people think that there is no witchcraft, but they fail to understand that witches in America wear a suit.

The spiritual atmosphere in Europe and America is thicker than in Africa. In Africa, it is easy to identify who a witch or warlock is and stay clear but in America, you can't tell. The innocent neighbor in America that you think is harmless may be the agent of the principality controlling that region. They may have scanned you spiritually and know that you are empty. When you go to invite them to church, they laugh, and you don't understand why.

Life is spiritual and prayer is the only way you can overcome darkness. Never underestimate the spiritual capacity of anyone because you don't know who they are or where they go at night. Not everyone sleeps at night.

Let me reveal something to you concerning spiritual structures and how it works. There are demonic structures in every part of the world and these structures control what is happening in the physical realm. Who do you think is the real ruler of your country? If you think it is your president, think again. This is the reason why Christians should stop fighting with one another concerning politics.

The real ruler of your country is a spirit, and the desire of that spirit is what is expressed in the country. The resultant effect is reflected in the political, social, and the economy of that country or region. This is the same thing with people coming up with divers' revelations saying that a spirit appeared to them. Some even open churches with such revelation and many people follow them. Who do you think is the brain behind the Greek civilization or who made Hitler be what he was? These are questions that when you ask, you will begin to intermeddle with spiritual things that will blow your mind.

Every country or region has spiritual forces controlling it and what they desire is what happens. They determine who is elected to high political offices and what policies or laws are made. For instance, in Africa, who came up with the idea that twins should be killed as soon as they are born? Who instituted human sacrifices to appease the gods? Who are these gods? Have you ever asked these questions? Some of the customs and traditions like new yam festivals, market days, when to not fetch water in a stream, and why a woman should not come out at night, or blow a whistle, who instituted them? Who introduced the masquerades in your village or the laws that govern your village? Daniel 10:13.

> *But the prince of the kingdom of Persia withstood me one and twenty days: but, lo, Michael, one of the chief princes, came to help me; and I remained there with the kings of Persia.* KJV

This passage reveals that there are spiritual forces that govern every region, and they are in a hierarchy. They are responsible for the laws and ordinances governing each region. Whatever wickedness or sin you see prevalent in any territory is because a spirit in control of that region is expressing himself. There is a spiritual ruler over a country and the ones that control states, local government, and villages, even your street. In Ezekiel 28:12, God was addressing the spiritual ruler of Tyrus that is the devil himself, the real king.

The same political structure you have in your country is the same spiritually. They even take it further by assigning rulers to areas or ZIP codes, streets and families. This is where familiar spirits come from. They know your family history because they have been in control for generations. This rulership remains enforced even when you travel out of your family compound. You cannot run or hide because your file is sent to the region you think you run to, and the spiritual wickedness continues.

HOW TO COOK PRAYER

There is no distance in the realm of the spirit, but spirits do respect territories. So, what they do is transfer your information to your new location and the spirit in charge of where you now reside will add to your affliction because you are now under his territory.

Every entrance to a city has demons at the gate. You cannot see them, but they are there. The activities at the gate of your city are more than the busiest metropolis in your country. The spirits know who comes into a city and determine what happens in their lives. This could be why some people cannot prosper or account for what they used their money to do despite working hard and living in that city for many years. Running away from your village because you thought a witch is bothering you is nonsense because as soon as you enter another territory, the demonic world knows your affliction and they may increase it if the spirit controlling where you run to is more wicked.

The measure of a spirit is not in size but wickedness so you should hide in God and generate power on the altar of prayer instead of running. A witch can put a mark on your forehead and that mark has signals that attract demons anywhere you run. Nothing is hidden in the spirit world so thinking that another location would be better is because you don't have spiritual intelligence.

I am taking the time to explain this so that you may see why you need to pray. Some people run to America for greener pasture but end up doing what they wouldn't do back in their country just to survive. The living condition of some people in America is sympathetic and because of shame, they cannot go back to their country. The people they left behind now live better than them in a country they thought was not good. It is not in a location but in a God who responds to prayer.

There is no other way to stop demonic operations in your territory or family except prayer. Prayer is the only weapon that will keep them away from you and the more you pray, the more their operation moves far from you. This will make you gain ground spiritually by amassing large territories where the demons ran away from. In the physical, you may be renting a house but spiritually you may own acres of land through spiritual control that you exercised. The reason why some people may hate you when you have not done anything to them may be because you have dealt with them through prayer, and they hate you for that.

This world is deep. Where there is violence or bloodshed is because the spirit in charge of that region wants blood. That spirit is expressing his desires. A spirit's desire includes lawlessness, violence, prostitution, incest, abortion, murder, robbery, pornography, theft, gambling, sexual perversion, corruption, drunkenness, and rape. Any wickedness or vices happening within a locality is through a spirit governing that place. Prayer is the only weapon that can stop these activities at least within a certain limit of your control.

Let me tell you why you need the power of prayer to function and excel in life. The devil is very powerful. You cannot be God's enemy if you are not a powerful being. God uniquely created the devil and put so much power and wisdom in him. If God were to allow, no Christian will be able to stand before Satan but the reason why he cannot harm you is because of Jesus. The devil used to control our galaxy and he had a throne. The Bible calls him a prince. It is because he wanted to be equal with God that is why he was thrown down. Isaiah 14:14, *I will ascend above the heights of the clouds; I will be like the most High.* The place that he wanted to occupy is where Jesus is occupying now.

The devil has not given up on his ambition, and he hates born-again Christians more because they are redeemed to sit together with Jesus far above him. At the same place he wanted to sit, the reason he tries everything to bring them down, Ephesians 1:21. If you have this understanding, you will see the need for prayer. The only way you can keep the devil out of your life is through prayer, and the more you pray, the farther he stays away from you. Remember, the principalities and powers, cannot be fought with natural strength but through prayer. I pray that as

HOW TO COOK PRAYER

you engage in prayer fervently, you will return with testimonies in Jesus' name.

Chapter 3

Why We Need to Pray

2 Chronicles 7:14
If my people, which are called by my name, shall humble themselves, and pray, and seek my face, and turn from their wicked ways; then will I hear from heaven, and will forgive their sin, and will heal their land. KJV

There are many reasons why we need to pray. God wants us to pray, He wants fellowship with us. Before the fall of man, God used to come down and fellowship with the man but when man fell, that fellowship can only be attained in prayer. Genesis 3:8

> *And they heard the voice of the Lord God walking in the garden in the cool of the day: and Adam and his wife hid themselves from the presence of the Lord God amongst the trees of the garden.* KJV

God wants to fellowship with man. This is one of the reasons He created man but when man fell, He could not because of sin. When you give your life to Jesus, that access is restored but you can only fellowship in prayer. When you pray, you have activated a long-lost relationship with God. This means that a prayerless Christian does not have fellowship with the heavenly father even though the access is there. Prayer is a lifeline through which we have access to heavenly provision. When you pray, divine supplies are shipped to you and continuous prayer maintains this shipping route. That is why you experience open doors as a praying Christian. Prayer is very needful if you want a breakthrough in life and your consistent engagement will make you prosperous on the earth. The following are some of the reasons why we need to pray.

PRAYER IS A COMMAND

God commands us to pray. God knows that the only way we can reach him as our Father is through prayer. That is why He commands us to engage in prayer consistently. *Mathew 6:6 But thou, when thou prayest, enter into thy closet, and when thou hast shut thy door, pray to thy Father which is in secret; and thy Father which seeth in secret shall reward thee openly.* God did not say if you pray but when you pray, this is a command; He expects us to pray. Prayer is an important part of our life else God will not command us to pray. It is the lack of this understanding that makes some Christians avoid prayer.

Prayer is communicating with the Father and if we don't pray, that means we are keeping malice with the one that holds our life. Do not sever the communication line between you and your Father in heaven, He wants us to pray to Him which is why He commanded us to pray. Imagine a father who asks his children to call him while at work so that he can know what is going on in the house. The children ran into trouble by locking themselves out but refuse to call their father because of fear. A call to their father would have given them access to where the spare key is but they were left in the cold hungry and tired. This is the same situation many Christians are in when they refuse to call on their heavenly father for help. God knows where the solution to every problem and challenge is, but He waits until we call. When you reach out to God in prayer you are obeying your Father's command.

IF WE DON'T PRAY, GOD WILL NOT ACT

Jeremiah 33:3, *Call unto Me, and I will answer thee, and show thee great and mighty things, which thou knowest not.* KJV

Know that if you don't pray, God will not act. As powerful as God is, He will be limited in the life of any believer who doesn't pray. God wants to heal us, provide for, and protect us but He will be incapacitated when we are prayerless. Imagine a scenario where someone is waiting for your call so that he can tell you where the key to provisions is kept. If you don't call, there will be no access. God waits patiently for His children to call on Him in prayer so that He can give them what He has in stock for them.

Someone may ask, why can't God just give us what we need without having to pray? Then I will ask you, will you reach out and give to someone who has no interest in you? Our first parent messed up so access to the heavenly provision is upon request. Before the fall, God used to come for fellowship without request but after the fall, you must reach out to receive, that is the way it is. If we want God to act in our lives, we must reach out to Him in prayer.

Let me tell you, God is closer to us than we think, the problem is we are not reaching out. Heaven is anxiously waiting for our call and as soon as we do, there is a dispatch. The angels on the switchboard of heaven are just waiting for your access line to beep green so that they can inform the warehouse of heaven to ship your package. But you are here running around looking for who will pray for you.

HOW TO COOK PRAYER

Prayer is a personal thing. I have never seen or heard that amazon send your package to another with your name. Your package that carries your name and address is always sent to you. If there is a mix-up and it mistakenly landed at another person's address, it still carries your name and address, and they always fix it with a refund or a resend. **Stop running around looking for prayer contractors whose address is on Facebook, pray for yourself.** Your pastor is not a prayer contractor, take personal responsibility and activate your shipment and there will be delivery.

If you want God to respond to any issue in your life, pray. You should love prayer not hate it. Learn to pray and you will want to engage in it always. The food that does not taste good is because it was not properly cooked. The moment you get it right, you will lick the plate.

Prayer when well-cooked will cause God to act in your life, Pray. The above scripture says we should call, and God will answer. If we don't call in prayer, there will be no response. God says He will even show you things you did not know anything about. It is a prayer that brings about discovery. Sometimes people we thought are friends could be hiding under the cloak of friendship and or family and oppress us. Prayer can reveal their evil agenda. Prayer can open doors that the enemy closed against us. Calling upon God in prayer will make God act in our lives.

ANGELS ARE DISPATCHED WHEN WE PRAY

Daniel 10:12 Then said he unto me, *"Fear not, Daniel, for from the first day that thou didst set thine heart to understand and to chasten thyself before thy God, thy words were heard; and I have come for thy words.* KJV

When you pray, angels are dispatched with answers. Daniel started praying and an angel was sent from heaven to bring an answer on the very first day. It seems that God is anxiously waiting for us to call upon Him. The reason why many are stagnated or suffer affliction is the lack of this revelation because if they knew how eager God is waiting for our call, prayer would become an interesting adventure. As soon as you begin to pray, God sends

His angel to bring the answer to your request. But you may ask why is it that many people do not receive the answer sent? That question will be answered as you go on in this book.

Remember we are talking about how to cook prayer. Before we finish this cooking, you will see why your answers are delayed or not delivered at all. But know that the response to your prayer is given immediately after you dial the heavenly line. Don't ever think that God stores prayer or looks into the matter you present to Him when He is less busy, no, God responds immediately. We are told in the bible that God is never too busy or needs an assistant. Despite administering the entire universe and the number of beings seeking his attention, He attains to everything without getting tired. Isaiah 40:28

> *Don't you know? Haven't you heard? The Lord is the everlasting God the creator of the ends of the earth. He doesn't grow tired or weary. His understanding is beyond human reach.* CEB.

Look at the scripture very closely, it tells us that God is never tried to attain to us. No matter the volume of your case, He attains to you at the instance of your call.

Also, the bible says that one hundred million people stand waiting for God to attend to them. I don't think there is any president that has that number of people waiting to be attended to. Daniel 7:10,

> *A fiery stream issued and came forth from before him: thousand thousands ministered unto him, and ten thousand times ten thousand stood before him: the judgment was set, and the books were opened.* KJV

God is always ready and when we call, He responds by sending an angel with answers. Keep the prayer line open and you will see the mighty hand of God upon your life.

NOTHING WILL HAPPEN FOR US IF WE DON'T PRAY

Mark 11:24 Therefore I say unto you, *What things soever ye desire, when ye pray, believe that ye receive them, and ye shall have them.* KJV

Friends, prayer is the one thing that makes something happen for us. Without prayer, nothing will happen. The Bible says that anything we desire, we should bring it to God in prayer. Do you want a husband or wife? Tell God in prayer and He will give it to you. If you want success or a breakthrough, it is only in prayer that you will receive the answer. God can even give you fame and fortune if you ask Him, Zephaniah 3:19. Our frustration in life is often because we don't pray and when we pray things begin to happen.

If you are attacked by the enemy or want an answer to a specific request, you can only receive it when you ask. Is there anything bothering you or do you need access to a divine secret, prayer is the way to go, and it will land on your doorstep. When Daniel was faced with the impossible, he went to God in prayer and the bible says that the secret was revealed to Daniel in the night after he prayed, Daniel 2:19. Imagine a king asking you to tell him his dream and then interpret else he will kill you. That was the most impossible request, yet that impossibility became possible when a man prayed. I don't think your situation matches that of Daniel therefore go to God in prayer and the same way God responded to Daniel, He will respond to you.

PRAYER CHANGES US AND THINGS

Luke 9:29 And as he prayed, *the fashion of his countenance was altered, and his raiment was white and glistering.* KJV

Prayer will always change you first before it changes things. Prayer can shift things in both the physical and spiritual realm but before it does that, it will first impact your life. It is on the altar of prayer that bad habits, addictions, and vices are removed. If you are struggling with any addiction, prayer can remove or stop the addiction before it changes things around you.

When you pray, God will show you things that are not supposed to be a part of your life and as you continue in prayer these things will be removed from you. The scripture above says that as Jesus prayed, his countenance changed. It is in the place of prayer that we experience a change in our lives. Prayer can alter you and transfigure you to a realm higher than where you are spiritually. If you have been struggling in your Christian life, prayer can change that. Prayer transformed Jesus and brought a heavenly vision that made others see who he truly is. When you give yourself to prayer, God will transform your life. Anger, pride, hatred, and grudges can be removed when we give ourselves to prayer.

The more you pray, the more negative things that do not glorify God in your life are removed. You will be changed into another individual when you pray. This will not happen overnight but as you keep cooking yourself in prayer, you will notice a change in your life. In fact, people around you will first notice that you are no longer the person you used to be. Prayer will change you.

After prayer has impacted your life, it will begin to change your circumstances and situations. If you have an evil boss who will not want you to work in peace, prayer can remove him or her. It is a prayer that you use to reprogram things to your favor. If someone has vowed that you will not get married or make it in life, you can use prayer to reverse that evil ordinance and have a glorious marriage and breakthroughs. If you have been submitting proposals without getting approval, you can end such an ordeal on the altar of prayer to secure immediate approval.

When you pray, things change for your good. If no man comes for your hand in marriage, you can use prayer to change that evil circumstance. The enemy will never back down so you need prayer to change things in your life that you don't want. Prayer can also go into your future and change things; it can organize favor for you or stop evil. If you don't pray, the person you could have prayed to become born again may be the person who will kill someone you know tomorrow.

Prayer today can stop evil tomorrow. The only thing you can send to your tomorrow is prayer. You can pray a bad leader out of the office tomorrow today. You can stop a future Hitler or Idi Amin from manifesting today. Do you know that you can pray for an evil child from being born tomorrow? If someone had prayed, maybe the world would not have had people like Joseph Stalin and Ivan the Terrible among others. That could have saved millions from being killed. Your prayer can change things tomorrow in your family, community, or country.

PRAYER MAKES US BELIEVE THAT GOD EXISTS

Hebrew 11:6 *But without faith it is impossible to please him: for* **he that cometh to God must believe that he is**, *and that he is a rewarder of them that diligently seek him.* KJV

It is in prayer that we know and believe that God exists. Prayer reveals God to us personally and brings us into a relationship with Him. The reason why many do not believe or refuse to believe in the existence of God is that they do not pray to Him. Those who believe in evolution only do that because they don't know God personally. The devil gave someone the theory of evolution because he does not want man to have a relationship with God. This theory has led many astray and eventually send them to hell when they don't repent from such beliefs. The belief in mother nature is absurd, mother nature cannot create itself. God is the creator.

It is not rational to say that man evolves from something and that everything we see in this world happened by mistake. That is preposterous. How can it be true that what we see in this world is a happenchance, and that there is no grand designer? How can you believe that? Yet you never thought about the Manhattan skyline in New York that it did not happen by chance. Somebody designed and built them. We human beings create something and take credit for it yet the things that were created by God, we say happened by chance. **If the creation of man and all that we see was a happenchance, evolution, and spontaneous, then the skyscrapers in New York City should have evolved from a stone after millions of years.** Is it not funny that until now we have not seen any monkey or ape turn into a human being?

HOW TO COOK PRAYER

Man creates robots and takes credit for it yet believes that he came from something after years of evolution. Those who believe in the big bang and the theory of evolution and promote such only do that because they refuse to believe in the eternal God who created all things, Romans 1:19-23. When you believe in God, you will pray to Him and the more you go to Him in prayer, the more you begin to know Him personally.

The day it is widely accepted that God exists and that He designed and created everything we see, everyone will begin to seek Him, and pray to Him. This is what the devil is afraid of, so he promotes the big bang and the evolution theory to keep many people, especially the so-called intellectuals from accepting the existence of God.

When you pray to God, you will believe that He exists.

Chapter 4

When To Pray

Luke 18:1
And He spoke a parable unto them to this end,
that men ought always to pray and not to faint.
KJV

Pray always.

Prayer is a daily thing. Do not pray once a week or a month and think that you have prayed. A Christian who prays once a week is prayerless. Don't feel spiritual because you attended a weekly fire prayer meeting. Prayer must be made daily. Many Christians pray only in church services, and they go through the week waiting till the next church service before they pray again. Prayer is like food; you must engage daily. I have not seen anyone who eats once a week, if we cannot starve ourselves of food likewise, we must not starve ourselves from prayer. Maintain a steady communication line with heaven to secure your life here on the earth.

The principalities and powers that are after you do not sleep neither do they go on break so you too should not go on break. Prayer can be made while you are driving, on the bus, or train. While walking on the street or taking a coffee in the shop, you can pray. You don't need any special time or place to make a prayer.

The Bible says that we should pray always and not get tired. This means that we should engage in prayer without stopping. That doesn't mean you should organize a prayer meeting, and nobody leaves, no, if you do that you will not be effective. I have heard some pastors say that until you pray for eight to ten hours a day, you have not started, or you are not a good Christian. You see sometimes people form a theology base on their personal revelation. If God told your pastor to pray for ten hours, that is not for you, it was specifically for him.

A businessman or student who spends ten hours a day praying, what time will he or she use to study or carry out his business? As a full-time pastor, it is your responsibility to pray long and study the word. If God told you to tarry long in His presence so that you can manifest in a certain gift or anointing, that is for you and not the church members. Remember you are at your place of work so spending long hours daily on the prayer altar is part of your job as a pastor. Do not put this on your members and make them feel guilty for not praying long.

When Jesus was about to be arrested and crucified, he asked his disciple why they couldn't stay awake and pray with him for one hour, Mathew 26:40. As a pastor, stop using your personal revelation to burden your members. It is important to pray and tarry in the presence of God but should not be imposed on church members based on personal revelation.

One day I went to church to clean, I saw my pastors and other church leaders rounding up a prayer meeting. Something immediately said inside me that we always come to church and pray and when we are done, we would go and work for those who do not pray or love God. I did not premeditate that. It was as if something fell off my eyes and I thought about that for a long time. Till today I don't know where that statement came from, but I know it did not come from me.

We Christians think that our dominion is in the church and so we occupy ourselves with so many activities and forget what God wants us to do. Jesus says that we should occupy till he comes, Luke 19:13 *And he called his ten servants, and delivered them ten pounds, and said unto them, Occupy till I come.* But we have seen that Christians are not occupying. Tell me, which president of a country is a born-again child of God; I don't mean churchgoer, but a genuine born-again Holy Spirit-filled? If you find any, please let me know. Which Governor of a state in your country or mayor or chairman is a born-again child of God. I have not yet seen a senate president, speaker of the house, or a supreme court judge that is a born-again child of God.

Our occupying as Christians is in the church but that is not what the bible says. While we spend long hours praying, the people of the world are taking over. When we are done praying, we go and work for them; and they make policies that fashion the way we live.

The time for election will soon come, which potential candidate is a born-again Christian? But during elections, born-again Christians will fight with one another just to support a non-born again and vote them into office. Many are even deceived into believing that a certain candidate is God-sent, and that heaven has endorsed the candidate.

During the global pandemic lockdown of 2020, a born-again president or governor would have taken a different approach because of his or her belief in God. They may have called for a national fasting and prayer meeting, and things would have turned out differently. But the people of the world have a different mindset. Do you remember how your political leaders declared a national lockdown and no church was opened or congregated? Did your pastor have the power to override the order? Did they not switch to online service until the lockdown was lifted? Our power as Christians should not be in the church, we should go out there and dominate.

Understand that political power is very important that is why the devil is mindful of whom he allows to have it. Luke 4:6

And the devil said unto him, All this power will I give thee, and the glory of them: for that is delivered unto me; and to whomsoever I will I give it. KJV

Political power is what controls everything that is why God wants us to have it. **A born-again president will do more for the kingdom of God than a pastor**, why? because he or she will use the power of the office to advance the purposes of God in the country. A pastor is only in charge of a few members, but a president oversees the whole country and what he says happens. A pastor who disobeys a president or governor's order could be arrested and jailed. Do you see why Christians need to be out there controlling things instead of spending long hours daily praying?

I am not discouraging long hours of prayer; it is very good and should be engaged when you are at liberty to do so. But if you are a politician, businessman, career woman, or student, you need to give in all your best in the discipline of study and other engagement that will take you to the top for God.

God wants His children at the management level in their careers. **It will be good for the kingdom of God if a born-again Christian is the richest man in the world.** Imagine how he or she would use the billions to influence policies and advance the purposes of God instead of sending rockets to space in search of alien lives or habitable planets.

While you are out there trying to take over, always be in the mood of prayer. Sometimes you can take a leave from work or business and camp with God and when you come out your spiritual level will increase.

The Bible says that we should pray always meaning that we should always be in the mood of prayer while we are out engaging in our daily activity. A thirty-minute break can be a great time to pray and shift things in the spirit if you pray properly. While you are at lunch or on the way to work or to submit that proposal, you can connect to heaven at a high frequency without anyone knowing. If there is a situation in your place of work or you went blank in the exam hall, switch to heaven's frequency and God will respond. This is why the bible says that we should pray always.

Organizing a prayer meeting occasionally is good but we should not make church members feel that because they did not attend, they are not praying. Prayer should be taught and encouraged on a personal level so that church members would not depend only on corporate prayer.

Since COVID 19, many church activities have gone online, this is a good thing as churches can organize units of online prayer meetings. This can encourage members to participate and pray. With this kind of activity, prayer will be made continuously and at the same time encourage members to live a prayerful life.

Therefore, learn to pray always, pray when you are having your meals and pray while you are using the bathroom. Every minute of your life should be engaged in prayer. Instead of spending time on Facebook or Instagram looking at posts that will not add anything to your life, pray. Prayer will benefit you more than empty talk with your friends or gossiping about others. A time spent in prayer will yield a great result than any other engagement.

The only thing you can send to your future is prayer. The reason why I am at this level in life is because of prayer. Years back, I used to wake up at midnight and pray for at least one hour. I will speak into the heavens not knowing that I was sending things to my future and programing my life. I would wake up again at five in the morning and program things into my future, I did not know that what I did had implications and today I am enjoying it. Nobody taught me what to say in prayer, but I was saying some heavy things that neighbors on the other side of the fence started to join me by praying in their houses. My night and morning prayer life affected others around me.

If you want to have a glorious future, you must engage in prayer always. Know that no prayer is lost if done right. If you are going to submit a contract proposal, pray. Don't think that everybody you see is a normal human being. While you are sleeping, some people are having meetings with spirits and shifting things in the supernatural and when you wake up you go to compete with them. **Life is spiritual and only those who interact with spirits stay at the top.** Nobody runs a business and succeeds without engaging the help of a spirit. Therefore, maximize your night as a born-again child of God else you will remain at the base of the ladder feeding on the crumbs that you call salary.

If you want to make a mark, prayer should be your faithful companion. The devil is out to frustrate the believers and if you do not pray, you will be a victim. The reason why many cannot go beyond a certain level in life is that they are prayerless. If you want to break through in your career or business, learn to pray always.

Anything you see or desire in this life can be procured on the altar of prayer. When you do business with heaven through prayer, life becomes a living wonder. That car or house that you desire is in the realm of the spirit and only prayer can bring them out. If I knew that what I was doing by praying consistently, especially at night will bring good things to my life, I would have engaged more. For your tomorrow to shine, engage the dark hours of today in prayer. If you wait until a special time to pray, you may not pray. The Bible says to pray always, so engage in prayer every time and you will receive an answer.

Although we are to pray always, there are times of prayer, Acts 3:1, *now Peter and John went up together into the temple at the hour of prayer, being the ninth hour.* There are selected times that are very important to pray. I believe spiritual doors are open during these hours. Peter and John went to pray at the ninth hour which is 3 pm. The prayer hours are, 12 am, 3 am, 6 am, 9 am, 12 pm, 3 pm, 6 pm, and 9 pm. These are the time you should try to at least register your voice in the realm of the spirit in prayer.

I will encourage you to pray during these times, especially between 12 midnight and 3 am. If you want to grow spiritually and have spiritual dominion, learn to pray at these hours at night. I said before that whatever happens during the day is determined at night. So, if you pray during these hours at night, you will begin to turn things around in all areas of your life.

I will also want to encourage you to learn how to pray long if you want to advance spiritually. It is important for a child of God to spend time in the presence of God. The longer you pray, the more you grow spiritually. You don't have to be a pastor before you spend hours praying. Spending hours praying should go alongside other prayers you make during the day despite your busyness.

I believe that by the time you are done reading this book, your prayer life shall be boosted, and you will develop a robust prayer life that will make the devil afraid of you in Jesus' name.

Chapter 5

Where To Pray

1 Timothy 2:8
I will therefore that men pray every where, lifting up holy hands, without wrath and doubting. KJV

You should pray everywhere.

There is no limit to where you should pray. You can pray to God while commuting to work and while flying in a plane. Everywhere is a place of prayer. Your bathroom can become your prayer hub, and so is your office or place of business. You can pray while waiting for the bus or standing in the street. The church is not the only place of prayer as many supposed. You are the church, and God wants you to pray to Him everywhere. If you receive bad news that demands prayer, don't wait until you reach the house or church before you pray. Right where you are, reach out to heaven and the answer will come.

Therefore, it is important to study the word of God because you never know when you will have need. If you don't know the word, when trouble comes, you will wait until you reach home and begin to open the bible frantically searching for what God says concerning the situation. That is wrong. Store up the word of God in your heart. So that when the need arises even when you are on the road, you can knock on heaven's door with God's will concerning the situation and the answer will come.

Make your office or place of business a place of prayer, and commune with God anywhere you are. The church is a place where we go for corporate prayer. If you make the church your only place of prayer, then you are set for frustration. Corporate prayer can only do very little for you. Sometimes meeting in the church is only to put a seal on the prayer you prayed outside.

There are so many things to pray about that praying in church alone cannot handle. Your challenges may not make the prayer topic, so you need to settle that with God outside of the church. Praying everywhere makes you have a prayer life and prayer life is what makes you an overcomer in life. Let everywhere be your prayer hub and you will attract lots of angelic activity around you. Remember a prayerful Christian is a winning Christian.

The devil is out to destroy lives, and every child of God is a primary target. Prayer is the only way we can stop him. When you are prayerful, you will prosper in everything you do. If you learn to pray everywhere, you will turn yourself into a portal where spiritual activities always take place. Pray everywhere. Genesis 28:12, *And he dreamed, and behold a ladder set up on the earth, and the top of it reached to heaven: and behold the angels of God ascending and descending on it.* Jacob was in a place where he was supposed to pray but he chooses to sleep and dreamt of spiritual activities. If he was a man of prayer, he would not have slept there but prayed. He later exclaimed that God was in that place and he didn't even know.

Make everywhere you are a place of prayer so that you will not miss God. If you sense any demonic activity where you are, instead of trying to leave, switch to prayer and you will send them packing. Prayer is very important so it must be engaged everywhere. Some people wait until they go to a specific mountain before they pray. Your prayer mountain can be your one-room or school bathroom. If you make everywhere your prayer hub, you will consistently interact with heaven on a high frequency.

Chapter 6

Prayer Duration

Mathew 26:40
And He came to the disciples and found them sleeping, and said to Peter, "So, you men could not stay awake and keep watch with Me for one hour? AMP

There is no time frame instituted for a Christian to pray. If we want to set a duration for prayer or how long a child of God is supposed to pray, we will cap it at one hour per session according to what Jesus said to the disciples in the above scripture. You can pray the whole day if you want to, and you can pray three times; or seven times a day. Daniel prayed three times a day, Daniel 6:10, and king David also prayed three times a day according to Psalm 55:17.

Some pastors have put unnecessary burden on their members, stating that they should pray eight to ten hours before their prayer could be heard. Some even said that if you do not pray for eight hours, you are not a serious child of God. This is not true because the bible, which is a guide in our Christian walk, does not stipulate a time frame for prayer. Jesus asking the disciple to wait for one hour did not set that as a standard because if that was the case, a Christian should not pray more than an hour per session.

Nonetheless, as a child of God, you should spend time in the presence of God. The more you spend time in God's presence, the more you become intimate with Him, and the more you become intimate with God, you will come out and not know that your face is shining, Exodus 34:29.

Our relationship with God depends on our intimacy with Him. This can only be attained in the place of prayer. That notwithstanding, do not allow a pastor to make you feel guilty for not praying for long hours. Many of the things some pastors impose upon their members are the revelations given to them, and they build a theology around them.

Prayer has no specific duration. Your need, circumstance, or reason will determine how long you should pray. Some people can go long hours crying unto God without looking at the time because of the magnitude of their challenge or what brought them to the place of prayer. While some could spend a few quality minutes and receives a speedy answer. When Elijah prayed for fire, it took minutes, but the prophets of Baal took long hours, and no answer came according to 1 Kings 18:26-38.

Most times, the reason why many engage in long hours of prayer is that they want to please their pastor or to measure up to show they too can pray long. **Prayer is not a debate, it is a business that you transact with heaven.** I often tell people that they should not feel spiritual because they prayed. I have not seen someone who feels spiritual because they accomplished a business transaction. You should take prayer to be a serious business that must produce results. I believe as a child of God, praying for one hour on your own should not be a burden, it is something you should do with ease. Anytime you go to God in prayer, you should always have what to say that one hour can easily pass by without you noticing especially when you are on your altar. When you love the Lord Jesus, you will always want to approach him in prayer and time will not be a factor.

So, understand that there is no time frame for prayer, you pray according to your issue at hand. Sometimes while you are praying, God will place something in your heart and you begin to pray about that and by the time you come back to what you wanted to pray to God about, the time is far spent. If you always pray for a few minutes, don't feel guilty, just build yourself, study scriptures and carry others along in your prayer and one hour will become a workover. From this book, you will learn many things about prayer and by the time you begin to engage in your prayer time, things will be different; you will notice that your prayer duration has increased.

It is important as a child of God to spend long hours in prayer. If you are busy because of work or family, the weekend might be a good opportunity for you to spend extra hours praying. Saying that there is no stipulated time frame for prayer does not mean that you should be a one-minute prayer Christian. When you begin your prayer with praise and worship then followed by thanksgiving, half an hour must have gone. You may spend at least thirty minutes to one hour praying in the spirit to build yourself up and charge your environment. After that, you begin to pray for the salvation of souls and the advancement of the plans and purposes of God within your territory. You then pray for your political leaders and those in authority. You further pray for your church members. For instance, you pray for the barren, singles, and unmarried. You also pray for the divorced and widows, the sick, and every other challenge that you know members of your church are having. Then you pray for your family and yourself. When you are done, you start spiritual warfare by binding, casting, declaring, and decreeing. When you are done with that, you speak into your day and command the day to work for you. Finally, you give thanks. If you follow this pattern in your prayer time, three hours will not be enough for you.

Also, you can spread your prayer duration. While on your way to and from work including lunch time are great opportunities to engage in prayer. If you are driving, it would be great to engage that time in prayer, and if you are on public transport, you can pray quietly within yourself till you reach your destination. The hours you spend during the day praying when added to your nighttime prayer may be more than four hours of daily prayer. This will make you have an effective prayer life. It also means that you give God four hours a day, of your twenty-four hours.

Chapter 7

How to Pray

Mathew 6:9-13

*After this manner therefore pray ye: **Our Father** which art in heaven, Hallowed be thy name. **Thy kingdom** come, **Thy will** be done in earth, as it is in heaven. Give us this day our **daily bread**. And **forgive us our debts, as we forgive our debtors**. And **lead us not into temptation, but deliver us from evil**: For thine is the kingdom, and the power, and the glory, for ever. Amen.*

KJV

Prayer has a protocol, and until you follow the protocol you may miss it. The disciples of Jesus were men that prays, but they realized that their prayer was not making an impact, so they asked him to teach them how to pray. I thank God that they asked if not we would not have the perfect pattern or know the protocol to answer prayer.

I started by telling you that everybody prays, and although everyone prays, not everyone receives answers to their prayer. God is a God of pattern and protocol and until protocols are strictly followed, answers will not come. The following are the protocols to follow if you want to pray effectively and receive answers.

OUR FATHER - GOD MUST BE YOUR FATHER

To approach God in prayer, He must be your father. Unless you are not praying to Jehovah God, but if you are, He must first be your Father before your prayer can reach Him. It is your father in heaven that you must pray to not some gods or statues. You cannot call on someone you are not related to. The access line of heaven is only open to a son or daughter, not an outsider. When God becomes your father, you can reach Him anytime. **If God is** not your father and you receive an answer to your prayer, another agency or civilization may be sponsoring that response.

God must be your father for your prayer to be received. As a father or mother, your children have access to you at any time. They can enter your bedroom without knocking and take whatever they want without any consequence, but a visitor cannot. Most visitors are limited to the sitting room while others are kept outside. If God is your father, you will have access without any inhibition.

You can only call upon God if He is your father. You may ask, how can I make God my father? The only way you can have God as your father is to surrender your life to Jesus, accept him as your lord and savior and that is it. The moment you give your life to Jesus and be born again, God instantly becomes your father. It does not matter what anybody thinks or says, this is how to start praying. Access to God is through His son Jesus otherwise you are wasting your time. John 14:6

HOW TO COOK PRAYER

Jesus saith unto him, I am the way, the truth, and the life: no man cometh unto the Father, but by me. KJV

Jesus is the only way to the Father; without him, you are certainly not praying to God. If you want to give your life to Jesus so that God will become your father, please pray this prayer after me in the sincerity of your heart. You must truly accept Jesus into your heart so, this prayer is not merely empty words, they are your lifeline to eternal life. Don't take it casually.

ALTAR CALL

Lord Jesus, I come to you. I know I am a sinner, and I believe you came and died for me that I might be saved. I accept you Jesus as my Lord and Savior. Thank you, Jesus, for forgiving me. Thank you for saving me. Now I know my sins are forgiven. I am saved. I am born again. I am a child of God; old things are passed away and behold all things have become new. In Jesus' name, Amen.

Now that you prayed this prayer sincerely, you are born again. God has become your father. You may think that nothing happens but my friend, your spirit is now a brand-new spirit, and the Holy Spirit of God is now inside of you. Welcome into the family of God. You now have access to God, reach out to Him in prayer and He will respond speedily.

HALLOWED BE YOUR NAME (PRAISE AND WORSHIP)

Psalm 100:4, *Enter into his gates with thanksgiving, and into his courts with praise: be thankful unto him, and bless his name.* KJV

To approach God in prayer, you must begin with praise and worship. You must enter in with praise else no access. You don't jump into the presence of God and start talking, there is protocol. The reason why many prayers returned unanswered is that the one who prayed violated the prayer protocol. You do not enter the presence of a king without first paying obeisance. To have access to the presence of God, you must pass through the gate with thanksgiving, and then praise will usher you into the main court. While in the court, you may still not be able to see the king and present your petition if worship is lacking.

Therefore, begin by first praising and worshiping God and access will be granted to you to enter His Presence. Praise and worship are very important because it sanitizes the environment and brings the presence of God to you. Sometimes the answer to your prayer can come while you are praising and worshiping God.

There was a time I was in a terrible situation, I needed help from God. When my prayer time came, as I lifted my hand to heaven and begin to worship, I heard the voice of the Spirit giving me the direction that I needed. Although the instruction was not what I expected because it seemed that God was taking me backward but when I obeyed, doors were open, and I am now flying high. God never takes anyone backward even though His instruction may sometimes seem so. The point is that my needed help came in the place of worship. I did not even pray when the voice came. Praise and worship are very important because it opens the heaven and brings God down.

Any prayer that begins without thanksgiving, praise, and worship is bound to fail. Always start your prayer with praise and worship and you will receive answers speedily. Now let me teach you when you want to pray, start by thanking God for what he has already done in your life. If you think that God has not done anything, thank Him for life and when you are done, bless His holy name. Tell Him how good He is and all the benefits he has showered on you. You can kneel or raise your hands and adore His name, say something good to Him. When you do this, you have opened the gate into His presence and whatever you say after will get immediate attention.

I pray that the Holy Spirit will give you understanding and help you in your place of prayer to know what to say to enter the presence of the Almighty God in Jesus' name.

YOUR KINGDOM COME

Another protocol of prayer is kingdom-mindedness. If you are not after the kingdom of God in your prayer, it will be a wasted effort. Jesus says in his word that we should ask for the kingdom to come in our prayer. The kingdom protocol here is a template for us to seek first the kingdom in our prayer for our prayer to receive a speedy answer. Mathew 6:33 says *But seek first the kingdom of God and His righteousness, and all these things shall be added to you.* We should always start our prayer first by praying for the kingdom of God.

When you put the kingdom first, your prayer receives immediate answer. Pray for the plan and purposes of God, pray for souls to be saved, and pray for your church and members in need. Look around you and you will see kingdom needs that you can pray for. When you start your prayer like this, you have heaven's attention.

YOUR WILL BE DONE

Prayer protocol demands that you pray for the will of God. This is where many born-again Christians miss it. Always pray the will of God if you want an answer to your prayer. One of the foremost wills of God is that souls should be saved according to 2 Peter 3:9. If you start your prayer by first praying for the salvation of souls within your jurisdiction, you make God interested in whatever you have to say afterward. God takes pleasure when we put His will first before our needs.

Furthermore, before you engage in a prayer adventure, find out what God says in His word concerning that issue. Don't jump into prayer without first taking the time to find out what the bible says about that need or challenge. The Bible is the will of God and every situation you may ever face has answers in the Bible. For instance, if you are looking for a husband, the Bible in the book of Isaiah 34:16 says,

> *Seek ye out of the book of the Lord, and read: no one of these shall fail, **none shall want her mate**: for my mouth it hath commanded, and his spirit it hath gathered them.* KJV

This bible passage has the solution tailored to that need of a life partner. So, you go to God presenting His will and you will receive the answer. If you are stagnated in your career without a promotion when you are due, Deuteronomy 28:13 has the answer.

As a business person, if you are not making sales or your business is not breaking through, Isaiah 48:17 is the will of God for that challenge, take it to God. If you have difficulty conceiving, Psalm 113:9 is the will of God that can change the situation. When you pray for the will of God to be done, you will receive an immediate answer to your prayer.

The reason why many are frustrated in prayer is that they are not praying the scriptures. It is easier to pray for the will of God than to shout and scream for hours thinking that you are doing a spiritual thing. God only has respect for His word, not a scream and shout. Learn to search for what God says in the bible concerning your need and or challenges and you will spend less time on the prayer altar.

Answer to prayer does not come from spending long hours but from telling God what He says concerning that situation. A successful lawyer is the one that knows what the law says concerning the issue not the one with much grammar. Search the scripture, load them in your heart or write them out and recite them before God in prayer and you will receive an answer. May the Lord give you understanding.

GIVE US THIS DAY (DAILY PROVISION)

God wants us to ask Him for our daily provision. It is a poverty mentality to think of what you will eat tomorrow when it has not come yet. You don't need to worry about tomorrow because we are entitled to daily provision as God's children. The word says *give us this day our daily bread.* The bread is for today not another day. This implies that we should not be anxious about what will happen tomorrow because God has taken care of it already. God wants His children to trust that He will take care of their daily needs. Our understanding of this will take the anxiety out of our lives. I have never seen a baby that worries about what he or she will eat tomorrow so don't worry about anything. Keep trusting in God and every day He will take care of you.

FORGIVENESS

Forgiveness is extremely important in prayer. You must ask God to forgive you of any sin you have committed against Him. **As a born-again child of God, don't allow anybody to deceive you that once saved remain saved.** There are many who lost their salvation but still think that they are saved. You must daily ask God to forgive you. Even when you are still saved, do not have this consciousness that you are perfect. You may sin against God without knowing so you need to consistently keep your vessel clean and ready by asking for forgiveness.

It is humility to ask God for forgiveness and pride to think that you are perfect. You can sin in your thoughts, actions, or words without knowing. Before you go to sleep every night, ask God for mercy because you never know what will happen. Teach this to your family members so that if the trumpet sounds or something happens, you will see them in glory.

But to be forgiven, you must first forgive others. Mathew 6:14-15,

> *For if ye forgive men their trespasses, your heavenly Father will also forgive you: But if ye forgive not men their trespasses, neither will your Father forgive your trespasses.* KJV

God will never forgive you if you don't forgive others. No matter what others did to you, you have done the worst to God. Forgiveness is a two-way thing, when you forgive others, God forgives you. This is the reason why many prayers are not answered.

Bitterness, hatred, anger, malice, and grudges are the hindrance to many unanswered prayers. I call them spiritual sins. Every other sin like fornication can easily be repented of because you know you did the act, but spiritual sins can go unnoticed and is very dangerous. Unforgiveness can keep a believer in one spot forever.

If you want God to answer your prayer, forgive whoever hurt you. Forgive your parent, husband, wife, children, neighbor, mother-in-law, and friends for anything they may have done against you so that your prayer channel can be open. Stop calling a line that is not connected. Heaven will keep your access blocked, and you will be talking to a telephone that was disconnected.

Now that you are reading this, search yourself if there is anybody that you hold anything against, call them or reach out and make amends and your access to heaven will be opened. I did the same thing and my life changed. I reached out to those who offended me, and my access was opened. Now things are no longer the same, I have been going from glory to glory since. If you cannot get them on phone, walk up to them anytime you see them and reconcile. Tell them you were hurt but now you have forgiven them. If they are hostile and don't want to listen, fine, you have fulfilled righteousness and heaven has recorded that you took a step.

Before you reach out, you must first forgive in your heart. Forgiveness starts from the heart. It is when the heart is settled the mouth will speak. You know you cannot deceive God. Genuinely forgive people in your heart and you will be surprised how they may reach out to you on their own. Sometimes the reason for sickness and diseases in the life of people could be because of unforgiveness. If you take a step to forgive, it could be a step to healing.

Learn to stay in peace with people, practice advanced forgiveness and your life will never remain the same. Many people including born-again believers harbor unforgiveness against their parents. Even if your father or mother refused to take care of you and allowed you to suffer, forgive them. Don't allow their past mistakes to keep you in bondage. I know some parents did some terrible things to their children but that should not make you hate them and refuse to forgive. Some people may even refuse to forgive a country because they were deported.

No matter who offended you, forgive so that God will forgive you. Don't go to hell and be punished alongside people who committed the worst sins simply because of unforgiveness. Many people will miss heaven because they refused to forgive others. So, reach out to your parent and family members that you have refused to talk to for many years and reconcile and your life will turn around for good.

Forgive your wife, husband, children and your neighbor and God will forgive you.

If you are a pastor forgive your members or fellow pastor that did something against you. Pray for him, and if he took members of your church to start his ministry, pray for him to succeed, and God will turn your ministry around to your amazement.

To know that you have forgiven someone, talk to them when you see them or greet them. Malice is a sign of unforgiveness, so avoid keeping malice. You may not be friends again, but anytime you see them, greet them and walk away. If you notice a need in their life, pray for them, and God will answer you first. This is the way I live, and I tell you, it works.

After you have forgiven others, forgive yourself. Many people have refused to forgive themselves even after God has forgiven them. If you don't forgive yourself, the devil will take advantage of that and keep you in bondage. Not forgiving yourself is like not forgiving others. It means that you have refused to accept the mercy that God showed you.

The moment you ask God to forgive you and you have forgiven anyone that may have offended you, God forgives you. If you continue to have condemnation in your heart, know that it is from the devil because God will not condemn you. Rebuke that voice of accusation and forget about it and move on. Don't allow the devil to keep you in the bondage of condemnation and you refuse to forgive yourself. No matter the degree of sin you think you might have committed, forgive yourself and move on.

DELIVERANCE FROM EVIL

You see, the devil is the last in this protocol. Our problem is not the devil if we know how to pray. If you follow the prayer protocol, you will worry less about the devil. Our understanding of the protocol of prayer is what puts us ahead of the enemy. The Bible says we should ask for deliverance from the evil one, yet it puts him at the last. This means that the devil is not important in the prayer equation He is less of a problem if we do things right. I pray that as we follow this protocol, the enemy will be silenced forever in our lives in Jesus' name.

HOW TO COOK PRAYER

DON'T USE VAIN REPETITION

Mathew 6:7 *But when ye pray, use not vain repetitions, as the heathen do: for they think that they shall be heard for their much speaking.* KJV

Many people think that saying so many things or speaking big grammar will make their prayers be answered. God is not moved by how many words we speak in prayer, nor will he respond to repetitions. Big vocabulary and oratory are total nonsense before God. Consistent repetition in prayer is chanting and does not bring answers. Some people are fond of shouting in prayer thinking that is the only way God will hear. I have heard many pastors telling their members to shout so that heaven can hear them. Let me tell you, God is nearer to us than we think. A simple quiet prayer can prevail more than a shout if it is done according to the will of God following divine protocol.

Therefore, in prayer avoid big grammar, don't keep repeating words and shouting is not necessary. Imagine you shouting some prayer on a public bus or while walking on the street, that will look stupid.

When you pray, let it be as if you are discussing with a friend. I believe as a child; you did not shout before your parent gave you food or paid your school tuition nor did you keep repeating the word food or tuition before they responded. This is the same with God. Don't keep repeating words in prayer: that is chanting. Learn to keep your prayer simple and direct. Talk to God as if you are discussing with your friend. Tell Him what His word says and what you want in a simple manner and your Father in heaven will answer you.

CHAPTER 8

TYPES OF PRAYER

Ephesians 6:18
Praying always with all prayer and supplication in the Spirit, and watching thereunto with all perseverance and supplication for all saints. KJV

Prayer is not a one-way road, there are many types. The knowledge of different types of prayer will help you to cook the right prayer. Different life challenges and situation calls for a different type of prayer. There is a prayer for a specific situation. You will never receive medication for an ear problem when you have a headache. There is a time for everything. When you want to reach God, you should know what prayer to offer.

If you keep dialing heaven's line with one type of prayer every time, the angel on heaven's customer service desk may put your number on perpetual hold. You should know what the issue or challenge at hand is and which prayer to make. When you are faced with a challenge and don't know what to do, there is a prayer to pray at that instance. In fact, **there is a prayer to make when you don't feel like praying**. Before you pray, know what type of prayer you are praying and the approach.

Each type of prayer has a different approach and the understanding of this will help you to cook proper prayer. There is a time for the prayer of supplication and a time for a petition. Sometimes a prayer of thanksgiving is needed whereas at other times prayer of inquiry, command, or praying only in the spirit. If you have this understanding and apply them accordingly, you will always come out smiling with answers.

If you are faced with a demonic challenge or an agent of the devil, that is not the time for supplication or thanksgiving. You should immediately bind that devil and command them out of your territory. If you sense things in the spirit around you and you don't know what to do, that is the time to blast in tongues. Meet situations with the right prayer and you will live victoriously.

PRAYER OF THANKSGIVING

Philippians 4:6 *Be careful for nothing; but in every thing by prayer and supplication* ***with thanksgiving*** *let your requests be made known unto God.* KJV

Thanksgiving is an important prayer because it is a prayer that can never go wrong. You cannot be wrong giving thanks to God. If you live a thankful life, you will be a highflyer on the earth. A thanksgiver will never be a complainer or murmurer. God hates it when we murmur but promotes anyone who appreciates and gives thanks. Thanksgiving is so important that The United States of America set aside a day just to give thanks.

A thanksgiver never gets stranded or lacks anything. Anyone with an appreciative heart will always attract favor. As a human being, when I give someone something and they show appreciation by thanking me, I always want to do more but never consider giving again to the one who didn't thank me. That is the same way with God. If you thank God for the little, He will give you more.

Learn to appreciate every blessing no matter how little you may think it is and God will shower you with more. No matter the issue or challenge, give thanks. It is only thanksgiving that will usher you into your next level speedily. If you lost a job, give thanks, because that may be the only way God can use to get you to open a business or transit into a new job that He prepared for you. But if you murmur and complain, you may miss it. Thank God at the level you are now and remain faithful without minding others and you will see the hand of God taking you to a higher level.

Thanksgiving is very important because it opens you up for more blessings. But if you are not thankful you may begin to do foolish things that will not glorify God. God takes thanksgiving seriously according to Romans 1:21 and 1 Corinthians 10:10, *Neither murmur ye, as some of them also murmured, and were destroyed of the destroyer.* When you don't give thanks, you will murmur, and murmuring attracts the wrath of God. I think it is better to give thanks and live than to murmur and be destroyed.

I believe that Thanksgiving is the most important prayer you can pray because even when you pray other prayers, if you are not a thanksgiver, God will not be happy with you. Everywhere and every day we see the goodness of God in our lives, and it calls for thanksgiving. If you live a life of thanksgiving, God will bless you abundantly because He loves it when we thank Him for His goodness and mercy.

I am an addicted thanksgiver, and this is one of my secrets to success. There is something that I do every time I move from one house to the other. After packing, I would prostrate on the bare floor of the house that I am moving out of and thank God for providing and keeping me in that house and neighborhood. Before I moved into the new house, I would also prostrate and thank God for the new house and for bringing me to the new neighborhood. I do this faithfully and keep going from glory to glory. If you saw me where I was before and where I am now, you will know that God is good. A life of thanksgiving will always lift you high because God loves a thankful heart. A child that appreciates the parent will always receive more.

Thanksgiving is an effective prayer that when engaged will bring speedy answers. Always start a prayer with thanksgiving and end with thanksgiving. Sometimes do not ask God for anything but simply thank Him for what He has done already. As you give yourself to thanking God always, I see the heavens open over you and your answers coming speedily in Jesus' name.

PRAYING IN TONGUES

1 Corinthians 14:2 *For he that speaketh in an unknown tongue speaketh not unto men, but unto God: for no man understandeth him; howbeit in the spirit he speaketh mysteries.* KJV

Romans 8:26-27, *Likewise the Spirit also helpeth our infirmities: for we know not what we should pray for as we ought: but the Spirit itself maketh intercession for us with groanings which cannot be uttered. And he that searcheth the hearts knoweth what is the mind of the Spirit, because he maketh intercession for the saints according to the will of God.* KJV

When you don't know what to pray for, pray in the spirit. Praying in tongues is the most powerful and accurate prayer you can pray. The first scripture says that when we speak in tongues, we are speaking mysteries in the spirit and only God understands. The most effective prayer any born-again Christian can pray is praying in the spirit. When you pray in the spirit, you are saying things that only God understands. The devil and his demons will never be able to interpret what you are saying.

HOW TO COOK PRAYER

Do you know that the reason why people are afflicted sometimes is because of the prayer they prayed? When you pray, demons hear you and launch an attack on those prayers but when you pray in the spirit, they are confused and wonder what you are saying. If you pray more in the spirit, you will be surprised how your life will turn out.

When you are baptized in the Holy Ghost, with the evidence of speaking in tongues, you have a new prayer language. If you use only this language to communicate with God in prayer, you will be far from affliction. Praying in the spirit is very powerful because it keeps the devil and his agents far from you. A Christian who engages in praying in the spirit will live an affliction-free life because the enemy will always run away from such. Anyone that keeps you from praying in the spirit is keeping you away from victories. To pray in the spirit, you must be baptized. If you are not baptized in the Holy Ghost, ask Jesus because he is the baptizer. No pastor or church should teach you how to speak in tongues. Praying in tongues is not taught but received as a gift according to Acts 2:38-39

> *Then Peter said unto them, Repent, and be baptized every one of you in the name of Jesus Christ for the remission of sins, and ye shall receive the gift of the Holy Ghost. For the promise is unto you, and to your children, and to all that are afar off, even as many as the Lord our God shall call.* KJV

If you are born again, the baptism of the Holy Ghost is for you. If anyone tries to teach you how to speak or pray in tongues, run as fast as you can because they want to lead you to destruction. As I said earlier, Jesus is the baptizer so you ask him, and he will baptize you himself according to Mathew 3:11. The second opening scripture says that the Holy Ghost helps our infirmity since we don't know what to pray for. Let me tell you, there are things you pray for and expect answers that are not what you should pray about. You can be praying for a car but that is not what you need. Instead, you are supposed to be praying against untimely death that the enemy has programmed for you anytime you get a car. When you pray in tongues, the Holy Spirit will then pray against untimely death and by the time you get a car, you will be far from an accident.

You see, many people marry the wrong person and end up regretting later. Others bought the wrong house or moved into the wrong neighborhood, and they are destroyed. We sincerely don't know what we should be praying about but with the help of the Holy Spirit, we can pray the right prayer that we need.

Once when I was in high (secondary) school, I went fishing and almost fell into a crocodile-infested river; an invisible hand held my back and gently pushed me to safety. I was so shaken and ran back home. When my mother returned from work, I told her what happened and she said that at the time the incident occurred, she had a nudge to pray. Since she did not know what to pray for, she started praying in the spirit. That was how I got helped. Heaven responded because my mother engaged the help of the spirit. Let me ask you, what prayer should my mum have prayed if she was not baptized in the spirit? She probably could have prayed a different prayer and would have lost a son.

Brethren, praying in the spirit is the most effective prayer you could pray and never miss. It goes to the heart of the challenge and produces a result. God loves us so much that he gave us the Holy Spirit and when we engage him, we live more than a conqueror life. According to Luke 11:13, God gives the Holy Spirit to those that ask, and Jesus baptizes you. So, if you are not yet baptized in the Spirit as a child of God, ask God in prayer. And Jesus will baptize you and you will begin to connect with heaven in a higher frequency that will keep the enemy far from you.

Let me warn you if you are faced with a demon-possessed person and you want to cast them out, do not pray in tongues. If you pray in tongues at that instance, the demons will not go out but will be held back because of fear. I have seen pastors and church leaders make this mistake. If you like, shout and scream, if you are speaking or praying in tongues, demons won't come out. Nobody including spirits wants to be burned by fire. When you pray in the spirit, your tongue emits fire and demons will be afraid. You only need to issue a command by first binding them and sending them back to hell. They don't want to go there but will not have any power to resist you.

Know when to pray or speak in tongues and when to use another type of prayer. If you want to operate in power, there is no other prayer except praying in tongues. If you spend time praying in the spirit, God will anoint you, and the more you pray, the more anointed you will be. Anointing may not come at a higher level when you pray other prayers like when you pray in the spirit. You can wake up at night and pray fervently in tongues or if you have time during the day.

Praying in the spirit is very important because it causes you to change your level spiritually, Ezekiel 47:4-5. If you have been asking God for specific graces or anointing to operate in your ministry, praying in the spirit will make it happen fast. You may not receive anointing or operate in a higher dimension of anointing if you pray only in your understanding. Gifts of the spirit and baptism into specific graces like the spirit of faith, wisdom, and the gifts of healing and working of miracles will come upon you quickly if you engage in praying in tongues. I would that you pray more in tongues than other prayers. May the Lord give you understanding.

PRAYER OF PETITION

A prayer of petition is a request appealing to God concerning a particular issue. This has to do with the court of heaven. In this type of prayer, you can write formerly on a paper. But your petition must be backed up with the word of God which is the constitution of heaven. You must quote relevant scriptures on the specific issue. Whether you are standing for someone, family, or yourself, you must be conversant with heaven's legal system. Remember the devil is the accuser of the brethren and he wants you to lose your case in the court of heaven. If you are not prepared, you can lose a case. In the court of heaven, there are people, and all of them except the devil are for you. But that will not translate into victory if you are found wanting in the application of the law. God is the chief judge of all the earth according to Genesis 18:25,

> *That be far from thee to do after this manner, to slay the righteous with the wicked: and that the righteous should be as the wicked, that be far from thee: Shall not the Judge of all the earth do right?*
>
> KJV

God is the chief judge of all the earth, and He presides in the court of heaven, but He will not judge in your favor if the devil who is the prosecutor has a stronger case against you. God is just and faithful. You must apply the law accordingly to secure a judgment in your favor. Jesus is also in the court of heaven as your advocate therefore you must come with knowledge of his sacrifice for you by his blood else you may not be helped.

In the court of heaven, there are the four beasts, the twenty-four elders, and an innumerable company of angels, all standing for you. But they may not be able to help if you are handicapped in heaven's legal proceeding. God is the impartial judge and the reason why He will not break the court rule for you is that He is faithful. That is why the universe trusts His judgment. Many people are walking around on this earth not knowing that a court sat in heaven concerning them and they lost the case. The reason why some Christians die untimely or are afflicted and limited in life could be that they lost a case in the court of heaven. Every day the court of heaven sits, and cases are read, and the accused are not present to defend themselves and they lost out. Remember the case of Job in Job 1:8,

> *And the Lord said unto Satan, Hast thou considered my servant Job, that there is none like him in the earth, a perfect and an upright man, one that feareth God, and escheweth evil?* KJV

Now Job was on earth having a good time and a court sat in heaven. God Himself brought out Job's case, and a legal proceeding ensued. The end of the matter is that Job lost the case and in the physical realm, he lost everything including his health. It was at the mercy of God that his life was spared. The case of Job should open your eyes to the court of heaven and put you on your toes. The prayer of petition is a prayer that puts you in the court of heaven to defend yourself or whoever you may stand for.

To appear in the court of heaven, take the case at hand, search the scriptures that relate to the issue and write them out. If you have everything by heart, that's good but remember you must present your case right with a good backup of the law. It is important if you write it out and treat it like a normal law court scene. When you are done, remember you will only be given access to the court through praise and worship. When you are done with the first protocol, approach the throne of grace boldly and declare your case. Tell God what He says in the constitution of heaven and why he should act on your petition. When you are done, end your presentation with praise and worship. If you know that the enemy is right and that you do not stand a chance in the court, plead the blood of Jesus. Your advocate will quickly jump to his feet and show God the eternal mark of redemption, and you will win the case. Heaven is a very busy place if you must know.

Let me give you a tip, as you prepare your case, ask yourself the question that God may ask you. Why should God respond? Why should He give you a child or why should that contract be given to you? Why should you be the one to be married this year? Knowing there are many eligible singles, who probably may stand a better chance if it was a contest? Why should you buy a house or get that promotion or win that election? These questions and others will help you to search the scripture to know what God says and apply them. A prayer of petition when done right will always secure speedy answers.

PRAYER OF SUPPLICATION

A prayer of supplication is asking God for something earnestly with humility. This is the prayer that sometimes gets people emotional, and they cry while praying. Understand that you do not beg God, but you ask humbly. A child of God doesn't beg just like your children don't beg you to get anything. Often this is done on the knee as you seek God's immediate attention to your need. God is the one that has the power to meet all your need or intervene in your situation. Therefore, in a prayer of supplication go to Him knowing that if He does not help you, nobody will. If you need anything, go to God in a prayer of supplication and he will respond.

The Bible says in Philippians 4:6, *Be careful for nothing; but in every thing **by prayer and supplication** with thanksgiving let your requests be made known unto God.* Whatever you want God to do for you, approach Him in a prayer of supplication and He will do it for you. When you go to God in a prayer of supplication, be sure that He is the only one you believe will do whatever you want. Don't pray to God and have hope in your uncle or friend. Your pastor is not your helper and certainly not your dad or mom. God is the only source that you should have and if your heart is fixed on Him, He will answer you.

A prayer of supplication may sometimes bring you to tears according to Hebrew 5:7,

> *Who in the days of his flesh, when he had offered up prayers and supplications with strong crying*

and tears unto him that was able to save him from death, and was heard in that he feared. KJV

Jesus offered a prayer of supplication to God with tears believing that God who is the only source would intervene and help him. Most times when you hear someone praying and crying, that individual may be offering a prayer of supplication and if you are close to them, do not try to stop them because at that point they are right in the presence of the Father.

Tears shed in a prayer of supplication are not premeditated but happen when your heart is open to your Father in heaven. If you are crying while praying because your situation hurts you or breaks your heart, that is not from the spirit. Thinking about situations and crying while praying does not qualify as a heartfelt prayer because the agency that sponsors the tears is emotion.

Do not try to be emotional when offering a prayer of supplication but be like Jesus who was overburdened with impending pain, and the weight of our sin; offered a prayer of supplication with strong crying. I did not know this at first when I use to pray and something from within started to fill my heart, till I couldn't hold it anymore and burst into tears. If you asked me what made me cry, I would not be able to tell. I was so overwhelmed and cried for a long time in prayer. The more I cried the more I prayed and couldn't stop on my own until the spirit is done.

A prayer of supplication will always attract the Spirit of God who will begin to do a work in you that when you are through, you will know that you touched something. If you have not prayed to this point, then you must build yourself spiritually because it is a moment that you can give anything to experience. With this prayer, things that are not from God that are in your life or around you will begin to drop off; and you will become spiritually empowered. This prayer often involves prayer for mercy and God's intervention.

PRAYER OF INQUIRY

1 Samuel 30:8 *And David enquired at the Lord, saying, Shall I pursue after this troop? shall I overtake them? And he answered him, Pursue: for thou shalt surely overtake them, and without fail recover all.* KJV

Mathew 7:7 Ask, *and it shall be given you; seek, and ye shall find; knock, and it shall be opened unto you.* KJV

A prayer of inquiry is a prayer that you ask God questions. In this prayer, you are seeking revelation, guidance, or a way out concerning a particular situation. In Jeremiah 33:3 God says *Call unto me, and I will answer thee, and show thee great and mighty things, which thou knowest not.* If you want a way out of a situation, you can call to God in a prayer of inquiry, and He will show you the way just like He did to David. The above scripture says ask and it shall be given, when you ask God, He will always respond. God is excited when we ask Him questions. Most of our challenges in life are because we lack direction. It is only the prayer of inquiry that will open the door to our next level in life.

The time for a prayer of inquiry is not the time for supplication or petition. You can ask God why things are not working for you or why a particular door has refused to open. When David was confronted with a difficult situation, he switched to a prayer of inquiry and God responded. God told him exactly what to do to change the situation.

In a prayer of inquiry, keep a book and pen by your side because as you are asking, God can open your eyes immediately to the reason behind the problem and what you should do to get out of it. For instance, you may be asking God why you are stagnated in your career, and He may open your eye to see that the job is not His plan for you. Rather, there is a business that you are supposed to do or there is another place you are supposed to be working. If you want to marry, the best prayer is the prayer of inquiry.

Don't be too excited and be praying for God to bless your marriage when you have not first asked Him if the person you want to marry is His will for you. You see marriage is not for today. What will happen in the next ten to fifteen years or more matters. When you sincerely ask God if you should marry the person, He will show you and His response will keep you out of trouble if you listen. Some people are afraid to ask God because they think if God disapproves, they may lose the person. But friends, is it not better to lose than for the person to leave you when you are getting old or turn you into a punching bag and probably kill you? Many married people are suffering in silence and the shame of being mocked by family and friends keeps them in bondage called marriage. Some people have lost their lives and destinies truncated because of who they got married to.

Learn to ask God questions and you will be free from trouble. I have seen many marriages that were celebrated collapse and husbands who left their wives when she needs them most. It is better to wait for God appointed person than to marry a man who leaves you when you reach the age that no one will look at you twice. As a man, do not marry a woman because she has everything that will make life good according to you.

Some men, instead of asking God to give them a wife, choose a woman who has a house, a car, and a child. If a woman has all these things, what then will you give to her? You should be a man and provide for your wife and give her everything. Your respect and honor will come when you are the provider, not a squatter. If you go into marriage because the woman has a good job or has money, you are a squatter. It doesn't matter that she is your wife. God asked the man to work the garden and not the woman, Genesis 2:15.

It is an error and reversal of dominion to live under a woman's provision. If it is for a short time for you to get back on your feet and begin to take responsibility, that is okay. But if you marry a woman because of what she has and you are comfortable that way, then you are in error. A woman was not supposed to work but the man. It is the prevailing economic situation that pushes women into the labor market. A woman should be in her father's house and be taken care of until marriage. When she gets married, her care becomes the responsibility of her husband.

By design, a woman is not supposed to suffer but is taken care of by a man. A woman's job is to take care of the home, it is a lot of work being a wife and a mother. Going to work for money is easier than being a housewife. Motherhood is too much responsibility. It is more dignifying for a man to be the sole breadwinner of the family. It is poverty that pushes women to look for a job. Some even take their newborn baby to another to take care of in the name of daycare so they can go to work. How can you give birth, and a stranger is the one raising your child?

Get God's approval in everything through a prayer of inquiry. Ask God if the school you want to send your children to is the right one because you never know what will happen there a year later. Inquire from God if the journey you want to embark on is approved by Him. If God tell you to take the train or bus instead of the airplane, you should listen, your status regardless.

HOW TO COOK PRAYER

A prayer of inquiry is the prayer that will show you exactly what to do and the steps to take to secure your desire. I live in New York and is very expensive. It is expensive to buy or rent a house and many people spent most of their income on rent. This makes a lot of people move out of New York to other less expensive cities. When people approach me to tell me that they are moving because the rent is too high, the first thing I ask them is if God approves of their leaving. You see it does not matter where you live, it is the God you have. God can bless you in any city regardless of the cost. If God does not tell you to move to a different city, you are on your own and if anything happens to you there, do not blame God.

You should inquire first from God if you should move and if He doesn't reply, do not take a step. God knows tomorrow and where you should be. You may be running away from an expensive city only for you to get into a bigger problem than the one you ran away from. I think it is a poverty mentality to run away from a city because of expenses. You should instead seek the blessing of God so that you can match the living conditions of the place. In the city you are running from, some people are building houses and making millions.

Always ask God for direction before you take steps in life. Someone may ask, how do I know that God has responded to my prayer of inquiry? If you don't hear God audibly, you can have a response from the scripture or people around you. Sometimes God can speak through your friend, pastor, child, or wife, and you must be sensitive to trap the signal when it comes. God speaks to me more from the scriptures. All my breakthrough steps came from opening the bible.

PRAYER OF COMMAND

Mark 11:23 *For verily I say unto you, That whosoever shall say unto this mountain, Be thou removed, and be thou cast into the sea; and shall not doubt in his heart, but shall believe that those things which he saith shall come to pass; he shall have whatsoever he saith.* KJV

Many born-again Christians pray but do not know when to issue a command or speak to situations. There are times you should get up from your knees and speak to the situation. A prayer of command is a prayer that the devil and his agents are afraid of because it puts you in the right office of man that God created you to be. When God created man, He puts everything under man's control Genesis 1:28. But when man fell, he lost that authority and dominion. When you are born again, the authority and dominion are restored but many do not use it. When you pray a prayer of command, you are exercising your God-given authority and dominion over creation. Everything on this earth is under your authority therefore you should exercise this authority frequently.

In a prayer of command, you are speaking to the situation. Mind you, everything in this realm both animate and inanimate has ears. You can speak to the sun, moon, and stars including the earth and they will hear you. Joshua 10:12

> *Then spake Joshua to the Lord in the day when the Lord delivered up the Amorites before the children of Israel, and he said in the sight of Israel, Sun,*

stand thou still upon Gibeon; and thou, Moon, in the valley of Ajalon. And the sun stood still, and the moon stayed, until the people had avenged themselves upon their enemies. Is not this written in the book of Jasher? So the sun stood still in the midst of heaven, and hasted not to go down about a whole day. KJV

Joshua was confronted with a situation, and he immediately issued a command and speak to the ordinances of heaven, and they obeyed him. He did not go on his knees and begin to cry and shout and ask God for help instead he exercised the authority given to man and got an immediate response. Moses also was confronted with a hindrance to the promised land, he went on his knees and started praying but God stopped him. He told him that is not the time for supplication but to issue a command and the sea will obey Genesis 14:15-16. Many Christians do not know the power behind the prayer of command. Sometimes you need to speak to the situation, and they will obey you.

HOW TO COOK PRAYER

Jesus says that if we *say* to the mountain. Is there any mountain-like situation in your life? speak to it. Don't ask God for help or go on long prayer, issue a command and they will obey you. You have the power resident in you, use it. That sickness that has refused to go after you have done all you can, speak and it will flee. Understand that sickness and disease are spirits, and they can hear; rebuke them and they will leave.

There are some prayers that you pray that are not needed, what you need to do is speak to that situation. See it as a mountain and it will move. Zachariah 4:7 *Who art thou, O great mountain? before Zerubbabel thou shalt become a plain: and he shall bring forth the headstone thereof with shoutings, crying, Grace, grace unto it.* Zerubbabel was confronted with a mountain, and he speak to it to become plain. Are there mountains in your life, turn them into plains by speaking to them?

There is no distance in the world of the spirit, you can stay where you are and issue a command to any part of the world, and it will respond just as if you were there. You can lay your hand on the ground and speak to the earth, and it will listen to you. Life is spiritual and only spiritual men with spiritual understanding rules the day.

I always stand in my room from twelve midnight or four in the morning and speak to the sun and the moon using the scripture in Psalm 121:6 *The sun shall not smite thee by day, nor the moon by night.* I would program things into my heavens in the womb of the morning and they obey me. I also command the morning, and the stars in their course to work for me. I tell the sun that I have risen before it, and as it rises to shine, it should shine favor on me and burn out wickedness in my heaven.

While you are sleeping, I program my day, week, month, and year and when we meet in the morning the lines will fall to me in pleasant places and I will have a goodly heritage. The first day of the year matters and determines how your year will go. You should program your year on the first midnight. Therefore, it is important to attend a church on New

Year's Eve instead of some wild party or staying home.

Brethren, these are the spiritual intelligence you need to have if you must reign in this life. Do you think I just woke up and started writing *How to Cook* Prayer? **Nothing just happens, everything is made to happen.** The enemy fought this book, but a higher command is what sustains the day. I have experienced unexplainable symptoms of sickness and all manner of attacks while writing this book, but God helped me through prayer.

As a child of God, learn to issue a command to a situation that is confronting you and life will be pleasant to you. If your child is sick and you tried everything and nothing seem to work, speak to the spirit behind the sickness and you will see your child recover immediately. God is waiting for you to speak to that situation and angels are waiting to carry out your command. Now that you know through this book, put it to practice and you will be amazed at the results you will have. I can't wait to hear your testimonies.

Apart from commanding situations and circumstances, you can command God. You may ask, can you command God? Oh yes, you can command Him, and He will respond and work for you. Here is the ticket in Isaiah 45:11

> *Thus saith the Lord, the Holy One of Israel, and his Maker, Ask me of things to come concerning my sons, and concerning the work of my hands* **command ye me.** KJV

God says you should command Him according to the scripture and if you do, you will have help. When the battle is too strong, and you don't know what to do, you can command God to take over the battle and your victory will be sure. In Psalm 68:1, David commanded God and said,

> *Let God arise, let his enemies be scattered: let them also that hate him flee before him.* KJV

David was probably on a war front, and it seemed his enemies were too strong for him. He commanded God to arise and take over the battle, and he got the victory. God Himself says you should command

Him and if you do, you will always have an upper hand over that situation. So, what are you waiting for? Rise and issue a command and things will turn around for your good.

PRAYER OF INTERCESSION

Eziekiel 22:30 *And I sought for a man among them, that should make up the hedge, and stand in the gap before me for the land, that I should not destroy it: but I found none.* KJV

A prayer of intercession is the prayer that you stand in the gap for others besides yourself. This prayer is selfless. The world needs intercessors, it needs men and women who can stand in the gap to bring about the plan and purposes of God on the earth. In your community, you can stand and intercede for the mercy of God. God says in the above scripture that He is looking for a man that will make up the hedge and stand before Him and your country, city, or state. Let me tell you if no one is available to stand for your community or family, the mercy of God will not prevail. This is the reason we see many terrible things happening and lives destroyed.

God is hiring intercessors; will you apply in person? The prayer of intercession is the prayer that will bring you to a level of anointing and breakthrough in a dimension you never thought possible. When you are an intercessor, God will always involve you in matters concerning your territory or jurisdiction. Heaven will not do anything without first consulting you. Genesis 18:17 *And the Lord said, Shall I hide from Abraham that thing which I do.* Abraham was an intercessor and God had to consult him before He destroyed cities within his territory. We see how Abraham interceded for those cities and because of that, his nephew Lot was not destroyed alongside the people of those cities.

If you don't rise as an intercessor and stand in the gap for your family, things will not change. You can rise to spiritual prominence through a prayer of intercession. You can do business with heaven as an intercessor and determine what goes on in your country or family. Understand that some men and women are the pillars of their country, states, communities, and family and nobody knows them but, in the spirit, their names ring a bell. The reason why some churches are still standing is not because of the pastors or board members, it could be one member that nobody knows, is the spiritual pillar of that church.

In a prayer of intercession, you bring the matter at hand before God and stand between, seeking mercy and intervention. If there is an evil pattern in your family, you can stand in the gap and intercede for God to end it. You may not need to involve anyone in a prayer of intercession, but when the result comes everyone will enjoy without knowing what happened. A group of people can also gather to intercede for their country, community, or church and bring the hand of God down. As an intercessor, you can determine the result of an election into political office in your country. Anything you see that is not good around you, you can stand in the gap and seek God's intervention. The easiest way to a breakthrough in life is to be an intercessor because when you pray to lift others and deliver them from destruction, God blesses you first. You can intercede for souls to be saved in your community and you will be blessed beyond measure.

But before you can become an intercessor, you must have love in your heart for people, for the things of God, and a burden. It is the burden that you have that will move you into a place of intercession. If you have a burden to see souls saved, it will move you to intercede for their salvation. This is what will wake you up at night to stand in the gap and intercede while they are sleeping or engaging in their evil acts. Your love for the souls of men will make you want to see them saved. Knowing that the wrath of God is coming upon all children of disobedience, you will want to see them get saved and so you plead with heaven for their salvation.

You can have a burden for your family and want to see things turn around for good. You can also have a burden for your church members who are sick, barren, or single and no man has come for their hand in marriage. These are a burden that you carry to your place of intercession and stand in the gap for them until you receive an answer. Many times, the reason why some people breakthrough in life is not because of what they did but because someone stood in the gap for them. An intercessor is not known but their impact is felt. If you are an intercessor, don't go around telling people that you are standing in the gap for them. It is a secret life that brings an open reward. Isaiah 62:6,

> *I have set watchmen upon thy walls, O Jerusalem,*
> *which shall never hold their peace day nor night:*
> *ye that make mention of the Lord, keep not silence,*
>
> KJV

An intercessor is a watchman, and they don't give God rest until He responds. Standing in the gap for a family or a nation requires consistency. It is not something you do occasionally and expects results. An intercessor must continue to stand between until the situation turns around. There was a particular situation where I stood in the gap within my territory, and the result was what I wanted. When that happened, I felt like I determine what happens within my territory. It was a good feeling, but you should be very careful because it can lead to pride and you know that God resists the proud, according to 1 Peter 5:5.

An intercessor must have jurisdiction before he or she could intercede effectively, especially when interceding for a territory. If you live in New York, depending on your spiritual authority, your county, borough, or village may be your jurisdiction or the entire New York State. The United States may be your jurisdiction if that is what is given to you. You should therefore not begin to intercede for Nigeria because that is not your jurisdiction. You can ask God to intervene in a situation in Nigeria because of certain connections like family or business but that prayer may not be as potent as someone who lives in Nigeria.

We should understand jurisdiction in a prayer of intercession so that we don't expend energy and valuable time on what we are not supposed to do. Your prayer of intercession may not be effective if you pray outside your jurisdiction. You can decide to pray for family or a specific area of need but when it comes to territory, you must have jurisdiction.

Know that Jesus is involved in a prayer of intercession as recorded in Romans 8:34,

> *Who is he that condemneth? It is Christ that died, yea rather, that is risen again, who is even at the right hand of God, who also maketh intercession for us.* KJV

The Holy Spirit also intercedes for us according to Romans 8:26. Intercession is very important that is why everyone should be involved. When you begin to intercede for others, you have become a partner with God in the administration of His plans and purposes within your given territory. Remember, God will not do anything without man's permission. **Intercession is therefore granting God permission to do things on the earth**.

A CRY

Psalm 56:9 *When I cry unto thee, then shall mine enemies turn back: this I know; for God is for me.* KJV

There are times we approach God with a cry. This cry can be for help or mercy. As a child of God, you should approach God sometimes with a cry. If you are too big to cry to God, then you may be too big to receive help or mercy. David was a king and a warrior who never lost a battle, yet he often seeks help from God with a cry. I have never seen a child who never cries for help from his parent. **No child is too big to cry, and unless you are God's uncle, you should always cry for help.**

There are times when we are overwhelmed with issues and challenges that the only way out is a cry for help. You should not be ashamed to cry to God. The Bible says in Psalm 51:17, *the sacrifices of God are a broken spirit: a broken and a contrite heart, O God, thou wilt not despise.* God will never despise a broken heart who cries to Him for help.

A cry for help or mercy will always get heaven's attention, it is a ticket to an immediate answer to prayer. I often cry to God, not because I force myself to. When I seek mercy or help concerning a challenge, my heart would break and I would be soaked in tears and when I finish, I wonder what just happened. Learn to cry for help especially when you don't know what to do and heaven will respond.

TALKING TO GOD

There are times you should not engage in normal prayer patterns but sit down and talk to God. Talking to God is a type of prayer that many are not aware of. I would that you talk to God more than you pray because the more you talk to God, the more personal He becomes. When you get used to talking to God, you will see your need met before they arrive. God wants intimacy and you can build intimacy with Him by consistently talking to Him. You see, in prayer, we shout and scream, sometimes we cry and yell but when we talk to God, we calm down and say things we might never mention in normal prayer. I have never seen someone yell at his friend when they are having a discussion.

The best relationship we can have with anyone is built on constant communication. The more you talk to someone, the more you are drawn closer to them or they to you. Husband and wife relationships can only flourish on the platform of communication. Where there is no communication, fighting and quarrel are bound to take residence in that marriage relationship.

Talking to God does not follow the rudiment of prayer although it is a form of prayer. You don't start talking to God by saying in Jesus' name. All you do is start a conversation as you would a friend. When you talk to God as you would a friend or earthly parent, you will be open and sincere. You can bring up issues and challenges and ask His opinion on steps you want to take. When king David went and sat before God in the temple as we learned in the previous chapter in 2 Samuel 7:18, he did not pray but talked to God. You too can develop this type of prayer by talking to God always. You can engage God in a discussion and one day, you will be surprised that He will talk back audibly.

Whatever your situation is, you can bring it to God in a discussion. Remember God is a spirit and when you interact with a spirit or summon him, he will come to you. If you build a habit of striking a conversation with God, He will be drawn to you. There is nothing too small that we cannot bring to God in a discussion. When you talk to God, you don't have to kneel but have a posture that you would when you are with a friend. Jesus is the best friend that we could ever have, and he wants to be involved in our lives.

God knows and understands our challenges because he was like us when he was here on earth. If you are lonely and do not have anyone to talk to, you have someone who is always there in the person of Jesus. God is not far away as many suppose but closer than we think. Sometimes we reach out to people thousands of miles away when we have Jesus who is nearer to us.

There was a time in my life that I was so lonely. I had no one to talk to and sometimes I would cry my heart out. But then on one occasion, as I sat on the staircase of the house I lived in at the time, wondering what to do, I heard someone speak to me quietly. It was so real that I turn to see even though the voice was not audible: what he said to me brought comfort that no human being can give. The bibles say in Psalm 46:1, *God is our refuge and strength,* ***a very present help*** *in trouble.* God is closer than our parents or friend. Since that experience, I prefer to reach out to God first before a human.

Learn to talk to God concerning every issue of your life. Don't keep feeling lonely and depressed because there is no one with you to talk to. Reach out to God and tell Him everything and He will guide you through. Remember when you talk to God, you don't need to start with praise and worship, or the name of Jesus and you certainly don't need to say amen after your conversation with Him. Reach out to Him as a friend and you will gradually build an intimacy with God that will make your life wonderful. This also applies to building intimacy with the Holy Spirit. Let me tell you, the best friend you can have in life is the Holy Spirit. This personality is not known by many Christians including pastors even though he is the chief executive of the body of Christ on the earth now.

The Holy Spirit is the one that will rapture the church. The reason why you will fly away in a twinkling of an eye at the trumpet sound is because of the Holy Spirit. He lives inside every born-again believer, yet they don't know him. What makes people give their lives to Jesus or cry during a sermon or worship service is the Holy Spirit. He is the reason why the church cannot be destroyed and why everything is working on this earth. The moment this personality is removed at the rapture, you would not want to be here because all hell will break loose. If you knew who the Holy Spirit is, you will want to make him your friend.

The Holy Spirit is the one who inspires me to write this book. Without him, I won't be able to write a single sentence. I am only a pen that he uses to write.

You can develop a relationship with the Holy Spirit and talk to him always. He knows who you are, what you want, and how you can succeed in life. He **the Holy Spirit holds the blueprint of your life** and when you make him your friend, he will lead you to breakthroughs and advancement that will blow your mind. Start a conversation with him, call his name all the time. Tell him everything including things you would never disclose to anyone, and he will help you out.

Remember that whatever you disclose to the Holy Spirit, no one will hear about it. He is not like your friends or pastors whom you confided, and they end up telling others or preaching about you on their pulpit. The Holy Spirit will keep all your secret and work to turn things around in your life. You will never be depressed or disappointed when you make him a friend.

With the understanding that you have from this book, stop telling people your problem, and stop making yourself a laughingstock. People are not to be trusted. You can tell them things in the sincerity of your heart thinking they are your friend, but they will go about telling others. Take your situation to the Holy Spirit and he will help you out. Make him your friend and you will never regret it.

PRAYER OF WARFARE

2 Corinthians 10:4, *for the weapons of our warfare are not carnal, but mighty through God to the pulling down of strong holds.* KJV

Ephesians 6:11-12 Put on the whole armour of God, that ye may be able to stand against the wiles of the devil. For we wrestle not against flesh and blood, but against principalities, against powers, against the rulers of the darkness of this world, against spiritual wickedness in high places. KJV

2 Timothy 4:7 I have fought a good fight, I have finished my course, I have kept the faith. KJV

Life is a battleground, and you must fight to live. The enemy will not let you go unless you put up a fight. Every born-again Christian should engage in a prayer of warfare because this is the only way you can succeed in life. The devil has an agenda to steal, kill and destroy and the only way to stop him is to fight in prayer. The above scripture says that the weapons of our warfare are not earthly. This shows that we are in a fight, and you must be equipped with a spiritual weapon to engage in the fight. Without proper spiritual armor, you will lose because your real enemy is not human. Paul the apostle said that he fought a good fight. He is making us understand that his entire ministry was a fight, but he succeeded.

To secure your inheritance and breakthrough in your business, ministry, and career, you must engage in warfare prayer as a lifestyle. In warfare prayer, you confront the enemy and contend with him. When the enemy fires an arrow at you, you respond by returning the arrow and firing new arrows to destroy him.

To pray warfare prayer, you must wake up at night. **Sleeping all night and waking up in the morning to engage in warfare prayer is like going to a party when others are returning**. The night is the best time to engage in warfare because these are the peak hours of spiritual activities. **What happens during the day was determined during the night**.

Before you engage in warfare prayer, you must be full of the word of God. **Spiritual warfare is a war of words, and the higher words will always dominate**.

It is important to know that a believer who is wordless may become a casualty in spiritual warfare. The warlock who sends evil arrows to you or your family used words and you can only return those arrows by the word of God. You do not pray silent prayer when you engage in warfare, nor do you plead or cry. But speak boldly, bind and cast, command and declare.

For instance, you can pray to break evil altars, silence every tongue that rises against you in judgment, and blot out every handwriting of ordinance written against you according to Isaiah 54:17 and Colossian 2:14. You see, these are the word of God, but you use them to fight your enemy in warfare.

The more of the word of God you have in you, the more you gain ground in spiritual warfare. When you sense the hand of the wicked in any area of your life or there is a persistent issue that defies every prayer you have prayed, engage in warfare. If you keep seeing an individual in your dream who wants to hurt you or your business is going down in an unexplainable manner, put up a fight. Seek for scriptures and gather warfare prayer materials and go to battle at night. By the time you return, things will begin to take shape and your life, family, ministry, and business will experience advancement.

PREVENTIVE AND OFFENSIVE PRAYER

Psalm 21:11 *For they intended evil against thee: they imagined a mischievous device, which they are not able to perform.* KJV

A preventive and offensive prayer is a type of prayer you take the battle to the gates of your enemies. In this prayer, you are not waiting for an attack before you respond, you instead launch an assault to foil the enemy's plan. A preventive prayer is to protect you and keep you safe always. In driving, we have what is called defensive driving. This type of driving technique protects you from getting into an accident. In the United States, you are encouraged to take the class to help you stay safe on the road. Most auto insurance providers require drivers to take the class if they want a premium reduction.

HOW TO COOK PRAYER

A preventive prayer is like defensive driving, it keeps you away from the arrows of the enemy launched every second of the day. If you want to keep your family and business secure always, you should engage in a preventive prayer. Many born-again believers wait for something to happen before they respond. In most cases, it may be late because the damage has been done already. If you want to live an overcomer's life in this end time, you must know how to pray a preventive prayer.

When you stand to pray a preventive and offensive prayer, you fire arrows to the camp of your enemies. You raise a standard against any impending assault and build a wall of fire around everything that concerns you, using the scriptures in Isaiah 59:19 and Zechariah 2:5.

You should never wait for the enemy to attack you before you respond. It is a dangerous way to live. Learn to pray a preventive and offensive prayer. This will keep you and your family safe always.

SAMPLE PRAYER

The following are sample prayers of intercession, petition, supplication, command, warfare, etc. Some of the prayers are direct from the scripture and are potent. You can engage these prayers to see souls saved, establish your breakthrough and dominion and bring about the plans and purposes of God in your life and a given territory.

1. Father, in the name of Jesus, let there be a massive salvation of souls within my territory, all through this year and beyond (mention the name of your territory).
2. Father, in the name of Jesus, let the light of the glorious gospel of Christ shine across this territory bringing many to salvation. (Mention the name of your territory or where you have jurisdiction as you have learned).
3. Father, in the name of Jesus, let everyone ordained for eternal life within this territory (mention) receive their salvation.

4. Father, in the name of Jesus, let no one die within my territory (mention) who is ordained for eternal this year.
5. Father, in the name of Jesu, rescue everyone within my territory (mention) that the enemy want to destroy through committing suicide.
6. Father, in the name of Jesus, destroy every veil the enemy has used to cover people within this territory (mention) to hinder their salvation.
7. Father, in the name of Jesus let every gang up of hell against the revival of the church within this territory be brought to naught.
8. Father, in the name of Jesus, open the door of salvation to every unsaved soul in my family.
9. Father, by the fire of the Holy Ghost, consume every agent of the devil that seek to hinder the advancement of the gospel within my territory.

10. Holy Spirit of the living God, take control of my territory and preserve it from every form of attack from the enemy.
11. Holy Spirit of the living God, convict and convert every unsaved soul within the harvest field of this territory.
12. Let God arise, let His enemies be scattered. Let them that hates Him within this territory flee before Him.
13. I declare this territory a no-fly zone for witchcraft operation in the name of Jesus.
14. I cancel every evil handwriting of ordinance written against me and my family.
15. Seven hundred meters round about where I live, evil shall not come near in Jesus' name.
16. I draw a blood line around everything that concerns me in Jesus' name.
17. The enemy shall not exact upon me, nor the son of wickedness afflict me. God will beat down my foes before me and plague everyone that hates me.

18. Let the way be slippery for my enemies and let the angels of God pursue them to their destruction.
19. Every strong man or woman from my lineage that has refused to let me go, Father, let them go for me.
20. Affliction shall not arise a second time in my life.
21. I speak to you earth, reject all that has made themselves my enemy. (Place your hand on the ground).
22. I speak to you sun, I have risen before you, as you rise to shine today, shine favor upon me and my family.
23. I speak to you the moon; you will always shine favor upon me and my family.
24. I speak to you the stars; you will always work for me.
25. I speak to you the wind; you will always blow favor to me and my family.
26. I speak to you the ordinances of heaven; you will always answer for me.

27. Everywhere my name is mentioned, let favor answer.
28. Every closed door, I command you to open.
29. Lift up your head o gates and be lifted up for me and the work of my hands in this land. (This is for your business and career in a given territory).
30. Everywhere my name is mentioned for evil, let the blood of Jesus answer for me.
31. Every arrow of the wicked fired against me, I return them back to sender. It shall go and destroy the sender sevenfold.
32. I shall not die but live and declare the works of the Lord in my life to this generation.
33. I am blessed and highly favored. The grace of God that makes a man to succeed without struggling is upon me.
34. Everything that I sow in this land, I shall reap a hundredfold. I shall go forward and wax strong and grow until I become great,

and those that were in this land before me shall envy me.

35. Father, enlarge my territory and cause me to prosper.
36. Whatever God has not planted in my body, let it be uprooted.

Chapter 9

Prayer Code

Acts 4:12

Neither is there salvation in any other: for there is none other name under heaven given among men, whereby we must be saved. KJV

John 14:6

Jesus saith unto him, I am the way, the truth, and the life: no man cometh unto the Father, but by me. KJV

The name of Jesus is the only code that gets our prayer through to God. The name of Jesus is not a punctuation or a religious addendum, but a code that connects us to God in prayer. When you pray, you are dialing heaven's line and the only way that line can get through is the name of Jesus. Jesus says that he is the only way to the father. That statement means his name is the code that connects heaven's line. You may now ask me what about those who pray in a different name? My answer is, if you are praying to God in heaven, your prayer must be routed through the name of Jesus. To call someone in the United States, the access code is plus one. If you put plus two it will not work. That is the same way if you want to connect to heaven.

Anyone who prays in a different name, is not praying to Jehovah the God of our lord Jesus Christ. Many people have been praying a fruitless prayer simply because the code was not used. The scripture above says that there is no other name given to men under heaven meaning that any other name outside the name of Jesus is not recognized. Do you want to call heaven for help, you must first add the code which is the name of Jesus, and you will be connected?

If you have been praying using a different code, you should consider changing else you are only involving yourself in a fruitless task. God loves us so much that he gave his only son to come and die for us. Accepting Jesus as your lord and personal savior will grant you access in prayer to God. Remember, as long as you live in this world, you need God, but you can only reach Him through His son. The provision has been made in the preceding chapter if you want to surrender your life to Jesus. This world is very bad, and a time is coming when we all will have to give an account of what we did in the body. The only way of escape to the eternal life of peace and joy is through Jesus. Forget what you were born into or what you were introduced into, Jesus is the way to the Father.

Christianity is not a religion but man's expressway back to the Father. It does not matter what you may have done, the love of God is always available, and you will be forgiven. Return to God by accepting His son so that you can start using the right code to pray. **If you pray without using the name of Jesus, that prayer is not to God but a different civilization.** Jesus is the only acceptable code to heaven's line. Be wise.

Chapter 10

What Makes Prayer Effective

Hebrew 4:12
For the word of God is quick, and powerful, and sharper than any twoedged sword, piercing even to the dividing asunder of soul and spirit, and of the joints and marrow, and is a discerner of the thoughts and intents of the heart. KJV

THE WORD OF GOD

The word of God is what makes prayer effective. If you don't pray the scriptures, your prayer will be full of empty words that carry no weight. For your prayer to be effective, it must be full of God's word. Praying the word is very important because it is what gets God's attention and causes angels to carry out what you want. Angels only obey the word of God and anyone who prays the word attracts their ministry according to Psalm 103:20 *Bless the Lord, ye his angels, that excel in strength, that do his commandments, hearkening unto the voice of his word.* KJV

It is important for you to study the scripture so that you will know what God says concerning every situation in your life. There is a provision in the word of God for good health and if your health is challenged, the smart thing to do is to call His attention to His word. For instance, 1 Peter 2:24 talks about healing by the stripes of Jesus. Use that to pray to God, and healing will come. You can also add Mathew 8:17 *That it might be fulfilled which was spoken by Esaias the prophet, saying, Himself took our infirmities, and bare our sicknesses.* Praying these scriptures is what will make God respond not screaming and shouting or crying.

God is not moved by tears but is moved by His word. In fact, believing in these scriptures and praying them can get you instant healing than running to a pastor for prayer. If you go to a pastor and that pastor is not full of the word, any prayer he makes outside the word will not do you any good. It is better if you take personal responsibility and stay on the word of God, and you will receive the answer to all your challenges. Pastors are humans and they need help too. **The most anointed man of God according to you might be having the most anointed problem that you don't know.**

Personal discipline in studying the word of God can make you live a more colorful life than waiting to see a man of God. The time you spend in a counseling line, if used to study the word will solve your problem. If you have been afflicted by the enemy consistently, the word of God in Nahum 1:9

says that *affliction will not happen a second time,* so you take that to God in prayer.

God says something very profound regarding how we should get His attention in Isaiah 43:26, *put me in remembrance: let us plead together: declare thou, that thou mayest be justified.* He says you should keep Him in remembrance of His word. Isn't that interesting? God wants us to keep reminding Him of His word. This does not mean that He forgets but He wants us to approach Him using the provision that He made available. This makes it easy to get things from Him.

THE NAME OF JESUS

The name of Jesus is what makes our prayer also effective. Jesus is the word of God and when you pray in the name of Jesus, you are applying two things, the name, and the word. John 1:14 *And the Word was made flesh, and dwelt among us, (and we beheld his glory, the glory as of the only begotten of the Father,) full of grace and truth.* Jesus is the word of God made flesh so when you pray in his name, your prayer becomes effective. Imagine you combining the name of Jesus in prayer with the word of God that you searched concerning the issue at hand, your answer will be quick. The opening scripture says that the word of God is quick and sharp. Jesus is the word and applying him to your prayer makes the prayer receive a quick answer.

THE BLOOD OF JESUS

The blood of Jesus is another avenue through which our prayer becomes effective. The application of the blood of Jesus is very important because it procured a speedy response from heaven. At the instance of the blood, the devil and his agents run away. Nothing can stand the blood of Jesus. The blood of Jesus is the last resort on the prayer channel. When the blood is applied everything gives way. Remember when the blood was applied in Egypt, the demons that supported Pharoah ran away and Egypt was thrown into mourning. Also, those that were held captive were spared from death and freed at the same time Exodus 12:13.

HOW TO COOK PRAYER

When you are confronted with a difficult situation and don't know what to do, apply the blood of Jesus and everything will give way.

Sometimes before you sleep, put some red wine in a bucket, pray and turn it into the blood of Jesus and sprinkle it around your house and that challenge will go away. This is called the blood of sprinkling. The blood is what makes our prayer also effective when applied. Therefore, in prayer, plead the blood of Jesus over that challenge and you will overcome.

Chapter 11

Heart Connectivity

John 14:1
Let not your heart be troubled:
ye believe in God, believe also in me. KJV

In prayer, make sure your heart is connected. The greatest threat to prayer is distraction, and this is the number one weapon the devil uses to destroy your prayer. Distraction has left many prayers unanswered despite doing everything right. When you begin to pray, the enemy projects so many things into your mind just to take away your focus.

If he succeeds, no matter what you invested to cook the prayer, you will not have the answer. This the devil does by bringing issues and concerns to your attention. Some of the issues and concerns might be legitimate but if you give in, you have lost the opportunity for heaven to approve your request.

The devil can remind you while praying that you have not called someone you were supposed to reach out to and the consequence that will follow if you don't. This may be true but not the right thing to do at the moment. Remember that when you stand to pray, you are right before God and nothing else matters until you are done.

God has a way of turning out everything to work for your good if you keep your focus on Him. You may even receive a call for a job you have been searching for and praying for a long time but picking that call will distract you from your prayer. Understand that a time of prayer is not about what you may be praying for but about you being in the presence of your Father. No matter the issue the enemy tries to present to you, it is to take you away from that presence. Some thoughts may also go through your mind while you pray but you must do everything to remove them from your mind so that you can focus. Don't pray and be thinking about your children or the food you are about to cook. Your new car, cloth or money should not distract you from prayer.

It is good to close your eyes when you pray so you won't be distracted. Switch off your phone or television set when you pray.

In church, prayer time is not the time to greet people or look around. I see this happen in church a lot of times. Even pastors are distracted during prayer. Prayer time is not a greeting time or a time to discuss or inquire about something. There should be no movement in church when prayer is going on, but I don't know how that is going to be possible in charismatic churches. A pastor should not use prayer time to look around to see who came to church or not but should focus and connect to heaven. It hurts me to see pastors and church leaders shaking hands and exchanging pleasantries while prayer is going on. We seem to forget that we are in the presence of the God of heaven and all actions are weighed, 1 Samuel 2:3.

God watches us at all time and everything we do are recorded both by angels and demons. We should be mindful of how we act in the presence of the Most High God whether in church or in our private prayer time. **Your prayer will go as far as your heart is connected.** Avoid distraction at every cost. Those pleasantries in the church are distractions and they block our prayers. In your private prayer time, remove your eyes from everything around you. The reason we close our eyes in prayer I believe is to avoid distraction.

God wants us to focus on Him while we pray so that we can connect. Imagine you discussing with someone, and his attention is not on you, I personally hate that. I always want someone to look at me every time I talk to them, and my wife asks me why. The reason is that when you look at me while we talk, I see you are paying attention and getting what I am saying. But if you look away, I feel that you are not interested. That is the same with God.

Don't be talking to God and be looking at your Facebook or Instagram to see how many likes you got from your last post or responses from your WhatsApp. Keep yourself away from every form of distraction. The devil knows how to get things into our minds while we pray, that has happened to me several times. While you are being bombarded with different pictures from the kingdom of darkness just to distract you, keep your mind on your prayer. Don't buy what the devil is marketing, and sooner he will leave you alone. Sometimes the devil will remind you of things that happened years ago and if you focus on that, your heart will be disconnected.

Heart connectivity is very important in prayer because the moment we lose focus, our prayer gets hooked and may not reach heaven. That is the agenda of the devil, and you must overcome in order to cook a good prayer. Everything might be going well but the moment the heart is disconnected, that line will jam. No matter what you are passing through, don't allow it to bother you to the point of distracting you in prayer.

HOW TO COOK PRAYER

The scripture says that we should not allow our hearts to be troubled. The reason why many are distracted in prayer is that they are troubled by situations, and this breeds anxiety. The Bible says you should not be anxious. Keep the problem aside when you approach God in prayer so that your heart can be connected. When your heart is connected in prayer, your prayer posture will not matter. You can prepare a good prayer, and everything is right but the moment your heart is disconnected, that prayer becomes a wasted effort.

Many Christians do everything right and spent time in prayer but the reason the answer is not here is that the heart was not in that prayer. If you are facing a serious challenge, try and forget about it when you are in prayer and you will be heard. God wants us to connect with Him and the moment we do, our answer will be given. As you engage in a heart-connected prayer, God will answer you speedily in Jesus' name.

Chapter 12

Prayer Pattern

1King 18:33-38

*And he **put the wood in order**, and **cut the bullock in pieces**, and **laid him on the wood**, and said, Fill four barrels with water, and **pour it on the burnt sacrifice, and on the wood**. And he said, Do it the second time. And they did it the second time. And he said, Do it the third time. And they did it the third time. And the water ran round about the altar; and he filled the trench also with water. And it came to pass at **the time of the offering of the evening sacrifice**, that Elijah the prophet came near, and said, **Lord God of Abraham, Isaac, and of Israel**, let it be known*

HOW TO COOK PRAYER

*this day that thou art God in Israel, and that I am thy servant, and that I have **done all these things at thy word**. KJV*

The most effective way to pray and get a result is to learn what I call the Elijah pattern. **The reason why God answered prophet Elijah by fire was not because of how he prayed but the way he presented his prayer.** Every Christian prays but not all follows the correct pattern of prayer. When you want to get a result from your prayer you must follow a specific pattern else God will not answer. There is order in the kingdom of God and when we follow the order, we receive the blessings. Elijah the man of God gave us a pattern to follow if we want God to answer our prayer and not just answer but speedily. The fire of God fell immediately Elijah finished praying as though God was anxious. The reason is that Elijah followed a pattern.

Elijah started his prayer by putting the wood in order. The beginning of a thing matters a lot and determines how it will end. If the beginning is wrong, the end is bound to be wrong. By putting the wood in order, Elijah taught us that prayer begins with putting the word in order. If the word is not put in order the prayer will be wrong. The wood in our case is the word of God Luke 23:31, and we must put the right word in the right order. You don't appear before God with a healing need, and you present financial breakthrough scripture. That is not the right wood. *By his stripes you were healed* should not be replaced with *I will go before you and make every crooked places straight*. Are those the word of God? yes, but not the right wood regarding the situation.

Learn to study the word of God so that when you stand before God, you should know which scripture to use that suits the situation. If Elijah did not put the wood in order, he would not have gotten a response and he would have been killed. The enemy will use you to make hot soup if you present the wrong word in prayer.

After Prophet Elijah had put the wood in order, he proceeded to cut the bullock into pieces. This is very profound because if the bullock was not cut in pieces but chunks, he would have lost out despite putting the wood in order. The bullock here represents the situation. You must present your case in detail and not vague or random. You must tell God exactly what you want and how you want it. Be specific. If you want a child, what type? Male or female. Hannah asked God for a male child, and she got it. Don't appear before God and say give me a child, a car, or a breakthrough. Specify in detail exactly what you want and how you want it. This is cutting the wood into pieces.

I remember when I was looking for a house and I went to God in prayer. I asked Him for a two-bedroom house in a quiet neighborhood with no parking regulations. I told Him that I don't want the house near the main road and the neighborhood should have responsible residents. I added that it should be in a place where I can park all my cars without a problem whenever I get home. My wife is a witness I got exactly what I asked for and more. The house I got has private parking for residents at no cost. This is New York where you pay for everything but when you are specific, God will always add more. When you pray, cut your bullock into pieces by being specific and detailed and you will get exactly your request.

After the bullock was cut into pieces, Elijah laid it on the wood. This means that when you finish telling God the specifics of your need, you tie the word of God to that need. Tell Him what His word says concerning that request. When you do this, you are laying the pieces of the bullock on the wood. Elijah did not keep the bullock on the ground or the bare altar but the wood. Your request should match the word. Remember you started by sorting out the word needed and now you align those words to the specific need.

After this, Elijah poured water on the wood and the burnt offering. This means that you should keep adding the word to the situation. The water signifies the word of God Ephesians 5:26. Keep pouring the right word to your situation in prayer to the point that the water of the word will soak that need.

The Bible says that at the time of the evening sacrifice, Elijah came near to pray. There is a time for certain prayers. If Elijah prayed before or after the time of the evening sacrifice, he would not have received an answer. You should know when to approach God regarding a certain situation. This happens in a lot of ways. If God had told you to wait upon Him, if you did not and offer prayer, it will not work. God prefers us to obey than to sacrifice, 1 Samuel 15:22. If God told you to have patience, putting the wood in order and cutting the bullock into pieces will not produce results. If God asked you to wake up every midnight and pray, if you don't obey, you will only waste your time.

Also, there are certain prayers that you must pray at night. If you are fighting spiritual battles, the right time to pray is at night. If you begin to pray during the day, you may not have your desired result because night prayer has a lot to do with spiritual contention.

When Elijah started to pray, he called God by the name that He is known, Mathew 22:32 and Exodus

3:6. If he called on another name of God, probably he would have failed. There are the names of God you can call for a specific situation. For instance, if you want refuge, you call Jehovah Nissi. The name of God for the situation will get you a speedy response.

And finally, Elijah claim that he was doing all that according to the word of God. You should be sure that you are presenting your prayer according to the word of God. When you are word full, the enemy will not be able to accuse, and you will be bold before the throne of God.

As you follow this pattern to present your prayer, I see you return with answers in Jesus' name.

Chapter 13

Prayer Posture

Mark 11:25

*And when ye **stand** praying…*KJV

There is no specific posture that we are bound to in prayer. Although kneeling symbolizes prayer posture, you are not bound or mandated to kneel before you pray. You are not required to kneel or fall flat on your face before your prayer is heard. When the apostles approached Jesus and demanded to be taught how to pray, Jesus did not give them a posture. In prayer, you do what is best for you. Some people fall asleep when they kneel to pray and so they choose to walk around. The most important thing is that you are not distracted, and you are praying. Do not allow anyone to tell you that you must maintain a certain posture in prayer.

The Jews in the days of Jesus had a pattern of standing in prayer and that may be the obvious posture today, but Jesus knelt in some instances. If walking around, kneeling, or standing to pray will work for you, do it. The thing is you must be fully engaged in your prayer. If you are praying for long hours, standing, and walking around may be ideal for you because your knees will grow weak or tired quickly if you kneel. If you are asking God for mercy, the standing posture may not suit the prayer but prostrating or kneeling is recommended. You see, different prayer has different posture.

I like to stand or walk around while I pray whether in church or in my private prayer time but when I want to ask God for mercy, I go on my knees because that is a sign of respect and honor to God. You can't be asking for forgiveness and be sitting; it is not bad, but it doesn't look good. Notwithstanding, it depends on where you are or your health condition. Therefore, choose the posture you like when you want to pray.

There was a time David went and sat before God in the temple to pray, 2 Samuel 7:18, *Then went king David in, and sat before the Lord, and he said, Who am I, O Lord God? and what is my house, that thou hast brought me hitherto?* God did not rebuke David for sitting before Him or refused to answer his prayer. This shows you that there is no specific posture required in prayer, but you do as the occasion serves you. Why did David not kneel or prostrate or stand? Why did he choose to sit? This will give you the understanding that you can appear before God in prayer with any posture that you think is appropriate.

However, you should not appear before God in a yoga posture, that is not Godly. You can kneel, stand, walk around, sit, prostrate, or even lay on your bed. These are acceptable to God.

HOW TO COOK PRAYER

When Jesus wanted to feed the five thousand, he did not kneel but stood and lifted the basket of fish and loaves to heaven. When he was at the tomb of Lazarus, he did not kneel instead he was standing but when he was at the mount of olive preparing for the cross, he knelt to pray, *And he was withdrawn from them about a stone's cast, and kneeled down, and prayed,* Luke 22:41. Jesus knew which posture to use when praying depending on the situation.

When Hezekiah received bad news concerning his health, the Bible says that he turned on his bed and faced the wall and prayed, and God heard and responded immediately. 2 Kings 20:2, *Then he turned his face to the wall, and prayed unto the Lord, saying.* God did not look at the fact that Hezekiah was lying on the bed, He responded immediately to his prayer. You see prayer position does not matter if you know what to do depending on the circumstance. Sometimes you can lay on your bed and connect to heaven at a higher frequency than someone who kneels. But no matter your posture in prayer, let your heart be connected.

Chapter 14

The Mercy Seat

Hebrew 4:16
Let us therefore come boldly unto the throne of grace, that we may obtain mercy, and find grace to help in time of need. KJV

Hebrews 9:5-7
And over it the cherubims of glory shadowing the mercyseat; of which we cannot now speak particularly. Now when these things were thus ordained, the priests went always into the first tabernacle, accomplishing the service of God. But into the second went the high priest alone once every year, not without blood, which he offered for himself, and for the errors of the people. KJV

There is what is called the mercy seat. The mercy seat is the holiest of all where we enter to obtain mercy. Until the death of Jesus, no one had access to the holiest place except the high priest. He entered once a year with blood to atone for the sin of the people. But when Jesus died, the veil that divided the people from the holiest place was torn apart Matthew 27:51. This signifies that everyone now has access to God. Because of Jesus, you can approach the throne of grace and demand anything, and it will be given to you.

The scripture says that you should approach the throne boldly to obtain anything you want. No matter what you need in life, go to God as a son or daughter and request boldly, and God will give it to you. Some religion teaches that you must beg God before He answers you. Unless you are not a child of God but if you are, go to Him with all boldness. God wants all His children to approach Him with confidence and trust knowing that whatever they need, He will give.

When you approach the mercy seat, know what you want and present it properly. A casual prayer will not take you into the mercy seat but a deliberately prepared prayer. Understand that the mercy seat is where the Father is, and to get there, you must appear through the finished work of Christ. You must be born again and receive Jesus into your life.

There is no human sacrifice that can give you access to the throne of grace but the blood of Jesus. In the Old Testament, the priest entered the outer court to perform certain ordinances but to enter where the mercy seat is, only the high priest had access. Now we do not have a designated human high priest here on earth, Jesus is our high priest. He paid the price for us giving us access to the mercy seat so all we need to do is appear.

But you cannot appear just like that because the mercy seat is the presence of God; you must appear first as purchase possession which is what gives access. Also, you must appear boldly. You should never appear before the mercy seat as a beggar. In the kingdom, we don't beg. Jesus did not redeem us to be beggars, so you must appear before God boldly and demand anything that Jesus died for. Never tell God *please* in prayer. Don't say *I beg you*, God. If you beg God, He will not respond. The scripture says you should come boldly.

Before the cross, the high priest used to enter once, with blood to atone for sin. But when Jesus died, his blood atoned for our sin once and for all. So, all we need to do is enter and obtain.

Many believers don't know this that is why they run around looking for who to help them. Jesus paid the price already, and all you need do as a born-again believer is to appropriate what he paid for. There is nothing you cannot receive from God when you approach the mercy seat. If you sin against God, do not run away from Him. Instead, appear before the mercy seat. Some people refuse to go to church because they sinned.

I knew some people who refused to attain a Sunday service the week they sinned against God. You should not run away from your Father because you sinned against Him. That was the mistake Adam made, Genesis 3:8. Do not run away from the one that can clean you from all unrighteousness. God loves you and has made all the provisions for you to live righteously. He says you should approach the throne of grace to obtain mercy and get help in time of need. No matter your need, including forgiveness of sin, is available at the mercy seat.

Our access to the mercy seat means that God is approachable, there is no stand-between. There is no man that God has put on this earth to represent Him. God is now personal. You can talk to Him and pray to Him directly. Anyone who claims to be God's representative is a thief, John 10:8 *All that ever came before me are thieves and robbers: but the sheep did not hear them.* Anyone who asks you to bring money or valuables so that he can give to God for you is only playing with your destiny. This also applies to those who demand money to pray for you. The curtain of the temple was torn apart; everyone is now free to go to God on their own. A prayer contractor is only preying on your ignorance. If you give somebody money to pray for you, you are only wasting your time and money. Prayer is personal, and God is personal.

The only designated advocate God has given to man is Jesus, and he is seated in heaven. Whatever you want from God, go to Him in prayer, and He will hear you. God loves you and is always anxious to see you approach Him. Your pastor is not a stand between, he is sent to teach you about what Jesus did for you and encourage you to serve God. If he does anything more than that, you should be careful. The throne of grace is always open, make an appointment in prayer, and you will obtain all you want.

Chapter 15

The Court of Heaven

Isaiah 43:26
Remind Me [of your merits with a thorough report], let us plead and argue our case together; State your position, that you may be proved right.
AMP

Summon me, and let's go to trial together; you tell your story so that you may be vindicated! CEB

We have already established in the preceding chapter that the court of heaven is where you appear to present a case. Here, we will take an in-depth look at the workings of this court. Many born-again believers do not know about the court of heaven or heaven's legal system. Our entire prayer process hangs on heaven's legal system. If you are not aware of the practices and structure of heaven's legal system, you may not obtain anything you desire as you are supposed to on the earth.

Before you continue reading, ponder on the eternal words of the scriptures above rendered in unique and proper terms.

When you appear before God in prayer, first you should understand that you are in a court and that your prayer is a case that you want God to adjudicate. **Every matter you present before God is a legal case**. What makes it legal is that there is an accuser, contender, or prosecutor who already tendered evidence contesting your payer.

In our natural world, you may hear terms like *I pray the court* in cases presented before a law court. Your prayer is a case, and someone is contesting that prayer and does not want the court of heaven to judge that case in your favor. This is the reason why God the supreme being who is the chief judge in the court of heaven, is now asking you to prove the merit of your case through a thorough argument to be justified or be proved right. The other translation clearly says *let's go to trial where you can tell your story to be vindicated*. The judge is telling you to go to trial. This trial is to allow you the opportunity to argue your case. There is no plea bargain in heaven. Every case goes to trial and your competence in the court is what will determine if you win the case or not.

To appear in the court of heaven, you must have all the facts at hand. You cannot afford to appear without proper preparation else your prosecutor the devil will make nonsense of your prayer and win you. Before you appear in the court of heaven, you should gather all your evidence and facts of the case and know how to present them. It is not enough to have the facts if you don't know how to present them. You do not appear before the court of heaven and be in a hurry to go out. God says that you should present the merits of your case with a thorough report. This means that you must take time to prepare what you are going to present before heaven. You should dig into the pages of the bible to gather relevant scriptures regarding the issue at hand.

When you are done, you now present them before God. You tell the court what the Bible says concerning the situation and why the judge should judge in your favor. This is the opportunity to tell your story according to the above translation. When you are in court, the angels are there watching and Jesus your advocate is listening waiting for you to finish arguing your case. They all want you to win the case, but you must first do your homework before they can work for you.

The court of heaven sits every day, but many believers do not know about it. Every day, the devil appears before the court of heaven accusing you and demanding that your blessing be suspended pending the judgment of the court. This he does, knowing that you are unaware of the proceedings and if you don't appear, the judgment may be against you. Therefore, it is important to pray the word of God concerning your situation every day.

The reason why some are not blessed is that there is a case against them in the court of heaven and they are busy blaming people. God says that for you to be vindicated, you must tell your story. Before heaven judges in your favor, you must argue your case. No one will argue your case for you, and if you don't take responsibility, you may not appropriate what Jesus died and received for you. Your five minutes prayer will not go a long way or turn the case in your favor in the court of heaven.

The reason why the devil is called the accuser of the brethren is that he takes everybody who is born again to court and contends their blessing. When you are aware of this, you will prepare yourself every day to counter him.

HOW TO COOK PRAYER

The knowledge that there is a case against you in the court of heaven, will help you to cook the right prayer every day of your life.

Chapter 16

Personal Altar

Mathew 6:6
But thou, when thou prayest, enter into thy closet, and when thou hast shut thy door, pray to thy Father which is in secret; and thy Father which seeth in secret shall reward thee openly.

KJV

You must have a personal altar if you intend to cook the right prayer. A prayerless Christian is one without a personal altar. Everybody uses something and as a Christian, what you should use should be cooked from your altar. I am not talking about having a secret or private room, corner, or table where you keep anointing oil and other religious paraphernalia, no. I mean you having a private prayer life that is separate from the church and family.

A personal altar is a personal prayer life where you take things to God on your own without any interference. Many Christians do not have private prayer time, they only pray in church and they do it religiously feeling very spiritual. If you don't have a private prayer life, you are only existing by mercy. **Every serious Christian must have a prayer altar, a time and place where they meet with God alone.** You will know if you have a personal altar or not, you cannot deceive yourself. The scripture says when you pray, you should enter your closet and shut the door. This is personal. This is what you should not share with anyone.

Your private altar should be your sanctuary and place of interaction with heaven. You may not necessarily need to have a private room where you go to pray but if you do fine. **The room or space is not the altar but your time with God is the altar.** Your personal altar can be waking up at night always to pray. When you do this consistently, you have created a portal where you interact with spirits and in this case God.

Anything you do consistently attracts a spirit and the moment a spirit is attracted, a hub is created. This becomes a portal that even when you are not there anyone can interact or have an encounter with the spirit in that hub. This is the same thing that happened to Jacob, and he woke up and screamed that God is here and I knew it not. Genesis 28:16 *And Jacob awaked out of his sleep, and he said, Surely the Lord is in this place; and I knew it not.* His father Abraham might have created a hub in that location, and he just stumbled into it without knowing.

If you wake up every midnight to pray consistently, you will soon notice that around the time you normally pray, something will wake you up. If you sleep back because of tiredness, not long something will wake you up again. What do you think that is or who woke you up? The spirit you have been praying to has come to interact with you and will keep waking you up to do what summoned him. In my house, I do not have a special room where I go to pray because my entire house is an altar. I walk around my house at night or kneel in my sitting room or lay on my bed and pray.

Everywhere in my house is a praying spot and I do this consistently. The day I don't pray, I will feel so bad, and it hurt me. I have created a hub in my house that at a particular time, something will always wake me up to pray. If nothing wakes me up, my wife will wake me up to pray and she will go back to sleep.

Your altar is where you can contend with the enemy and receive everything you want or desire. Whatever battle you are fighting in life, you can overcome in your personal altar. It is your altar that you present your request to God or contend with the accuser in the court of heaven. While people in the world are cooking themselves in an evil pot, it is your altar where you too can cook yourself. Remember that we are cooking prayer and the only place where you can cook a proper prayer meal is your prayer altar. Take your personal altar to be your private kitchen, you can cook anything without anybody bothering or distracting you.

Prayer is the most potent love potion you can give to anyone, and it is in your altar that you can concoct that love portion; and when you come out, your spouse will love you more every day and people will wonder why. If you are a single lady looking for a husband, you can spray yourself with prayer perfume from your altar, and men will be attracted to you that you will need to ask your pastor to help you choose. You don't need to beg anyone to marry you, love you, or do something for you. Just take their names to your altar and they will favor you without knowing why. Anytime you are faced with a challenge or difficult situation, you take them to your altar, and by the time you come out that issue will become a workover. Your altar is your place of refuge, this is where you bring covering over you, your family, and your business.

Chapter 17

Family Altar

Genesis 18:19

For I know him, that he will command his children and his household after him, and they shall keep the way of the Lord, to do justice and judgment; that the Lord may bring upon Abraham that which he hath spoken of him. KJV

Every Christian family must have a family altar. Your family altar is your first line of defense against all assaults of the devil. It is when your family altar cannot handle the issue that you engage a higher altar which is the church. If you want your family to succeed and be covered from the evil that is spreading every day across the nations of the earth, then you must have a family altar. Your family altar is a place of refuge for your entire family. Whatever challenge any member of your family is facing can be overcome at the family altar.

A family altar is where your family meets every day before going to bed at night and early in the morning. If you want your children to turn out well, raise them on a family altar. If you want your marriage to work and your home to be peaceful, have a family altar.

There is a saying that a family that prays together stays together, this is true. When you meet every day praying as a family there is no way the devil will have access to destroy that family. God says that He knows Abraham will command his children and the entire household to serve Him. You cannot claim to be in charge of your family if you don't have a family prayer altar.

Your family prayer altar will help to put your family in check and keep everyone on the right path. When your family members know that there is a particular time that the family meets to pray at night, no one will need to be pursued to return home early. Your teenage son or daughter that stays out late even though you are a pastor, deacon, or elder in the church is because you don't have control over them. If you have a strictly instituted family prayer time, everyone will return home early.

Also, your family altar is a place where the family meets every day to interact and know how each other's day went. When you meet every day to pray and interact, there will be love and a strong bond that if one member is away, they will miss the moments.

Families need to have prayer time because it builds their faith, keeps them together, and makes everyone value each other. In some families, parents may not see the children eye to eye or interact because everyone is busy. Some return home at night or spend time in their room without fellowshipping with one another. The family altar can eradicate this as everyone is mandated to assemble at a particular time of the night.

Apart from meeting at night before going to sleep, the family altar requires that you pray early in the morning to commit the family into the hands of God. In our busy lives where we wake up early in the morning to meet up with the day's appointed, a Christian family must pray together before leaving the house. Your covering for the day as a family depends on your morning family devotion. You should set a time early in the morning where your family meets to pray without being in a hurry. This will instill discipline in the family and bring protection.

Whether in the morning or night, have a specific time, and draw a program where everyone is involved in the prayer. Even if you are a pastor, allow your family members to learn how to teach the word and lead a prayer. If you have children, this is the best way to raise them in a godly way. You can draw a rooster where each person in the family has a role to play. They should pick a bible passage base on a lesson and teach it in turn. Everyone should be given a prayer to lead and before you know it, they will develop an interest in the things of the Lord. If you build a family altar and practice this consistently, you will raise godly children. Also, love will continue to flow in your family and marital peace will become your eternal partner. May the Lord give you understanding and grant you the grace to be consistent in Jesus' name.

Chapter 18

Priesthood

Leviticus 6:12-13
*And the fire upon the altar shall be burning in it; it shall not be put out: and **the priest** shall burn wood on it every morning, and lay the burnt offering in order upon it; and he shall burn thereon the fat of the peace offerings. The fire shall ever be burning upon the altar; it shall never go out.* KJV

Every man should be a priest of his home and family. In this chapter, I will speak strictly to the men. A woman can become a priest of the family where a man is absent as in the case of a single parent. But where there are both parents, it is the responsibility of the man to become the priest of the family. Let me inform you that if anything goes wrong in the family, the man is to blame. The man should be the one to make sure that the fire on the altar burns consistently and as a priest, he should not allow it to go out. While your family is sleeping at night, you as the man should stand up and pray; this is your job. You don't need to involve your wife or children. Allow them to sleep but you should stand and legislate on behalf of your family.

If anything happens to your wife and children, it is because you are not taking responsibility. You should wake up at night and go around the house praying. You can go and lay hands on your wife and children one by one praying without them knowing about it. If your wife wakes up and wants to join you, tell her not to bother because it is a fight only for men. The reason why many families suffer molestation of sickness and misfortune is that the man sleeps too much and is not taking responsibility. It doesn't matter if you are a pastor or bishop, you must be the priest of your family.

In 1 Chronicles 16:43 David finished ministering to the people but still returned home to bless his family. This is the character of a priest. You should be the one to make sure that your family is secured spiritually. You cannot claim to be the head of the family and the man of the house when you cannot stand as a priest.

Priesthood is very important because it gives you an office to legislate spiritually over your family. You are the covering over your family and the spiritual atmosphere of your family depends on you. If you fail in your priesthood, your family becomes vulnerable and susceptible to demonic attack and assault. The scripture says that the fire on the altar should keep burning and as a priest you should put wood on that altar every morning and night to keep it burning. This is an office and a job.

For the sake of your family, you the man should keep the family altar fire burning. The wood in my opinion is the consistency of your prayer. When you stop praying, the fire will go dim and the longer you stop praying the dimmer the fire until it goes out. The Bible says that you should try all that you can to keep the fire burning. Your duty as the priest of your family is to stand upon your watch at night praying for your family and you do this as long as you live. Your family's protection and blessings hang on your priesthood. Do not think that having a family prayer time or altar is enough because if you do not exercise your priesthood, the damage the enemy will do will be great. If you did not know that you are the priest of your family, ask God for forgiveness and start.

Gone are the days when men sent the women to church and the women were the ones carrying the spiritual burden of the family. The man is not only the breadwinner of the family but also the family priest. Your prayer is what heaven is waiting for and anytime you raise your voice to pray, heaven honors it. Your voice may not have been heard that is why some unpleasant things are happening. You don't need to be running around asking your pastor to pray for your family. You must take up your official role as a priest and engage heaven for the sake of your wife and children. Your wife has done enough for the family, it is time she rests while you take up your role. Your children depend on your priesthood to succeed, and you need your priesthood to give a better life to your family.

Remember being a born-again-believing man makes you the priest of your family and it has nothing to do with your wife. It is what you must do. When Jacob was to confront Esau, he went into priesthood that night by telling his wives and children to go ahead while he performs the duty of his office, Genesis 32:22-24.

The priesthood will always require that you the man be left alone to wrestle and contend for the family. If you want to enjoy the blessings that God has for your family, be the priest of your home. The intensity of your priesthood will result in the buoyancy of your family. Your family's spiritual and physical health depends largely on your priesthood. You can carry this priesthood to your office or place of business by always standing in the gap for your family. Pray for them and you will see the hand of God mightily upon your family, and the enemy will not be able to have access.

SAMPLE PRAYER FOR YOUR FAMILY

Lay your hand upon your wife and child and say this prayer over them, especially at night while they are sleeping. It is fine if you just read the prayer over your wife and child. The prayers are scriptures. They are the potent word of God that will transform and bless your family.

1. I cover you with the blood of Jesus.
2. I plead the blood of Jesus over your life and destiny.
3. The enemy shall not exact upon you, nor the son of wickedness afflict you. God will beat down your foes before you, and plague everyone that hates you.
4. May the Lord bless you and keep you, may he be gracious unto you.
5. Let the light of God's countenance continue to shine upon you.

6. You shall be ten times better than your pears (for your child/children)
7. You shall be preferred above your contemporary (for your child/children)
8. May the grace of God that makes a man to succeed without struggling be upon you.
9. You shall be great (for your child/children)
10. You will not fail God, you will not fail destiny (for your child/children)
11. You shall never be a victim of circumstance.
12. You will always be at the right place at the right time.
13. Evil will happen before you get there and after you left, but none shall come near you.
14. The seed of the righteous shall be mighty, the generation of the upright shall be blessed (for your child/children).
15. You are a fruitful vine, you shall be fruitful (for your wife)
16. Your children shall rise and call you blessed (For your wife)

17. Anywhere your name is called for evil, the blood of Jesus answer for you, and it backfire.
18. Anywhere your name is mentioned, favor will answer.
19. Anyone that looks at you with an evil eye, it backfires.
20. Every arrow projected against your life and destiny; I return them back to sender.
21. I break every yoke of darkness upon your life.
22. Evil shall never come near you nor overtake you.
23. God shall be a wall of fire around you.
24. May the angels of God go with you everywhere you appear.
25. You shall succeed.
26. Nothing shall fail in your hand.
27. May God, grant you favor and speed
28. Your feet shall be like hind's feet, you shall walk in your high places (anoint your child/children's feet to pray this prayer).

29. You shall always dip your feet in oil (this is for the prosperity of your children).
30. You shall never be a concern but a blessing (for your child/children).
31. You will not miss rapture; you shall hear the trumpet sound.
32. You shall serve God all the days of your life.
33. You shall be discreet and wise.
34. Every weapon fashion against you shall not prosper. Every tongue that rises against you in judgement, I condemn.
35. Every handwriting of ordinance written against you; I blot them out by the blood of Jesus.

Chapter 19

The Power of Intercession

Ephesians 6:18
With all prayer and petition pray [with specific requests] at all times [on every occasion and in every season] in the Spirit, and with this in view, stay alert with all perseverance and petition **[interceding in prayer] for all** [a]***God's people.***
AMP

Colossians 1:9
For this cause we also, since the day we heard it, ***do not cease to pray for you****, and to desire that ye might be filled with the knowledge of his will in all wisdom and spiritual understanding;* KJV

HOW TO COOK PRAYER

We are to intercede for one another as God's children. And not only for our brethren but for our country, community, church, and the unsaved. It is the will of God that we intercede for others. A prayer of intercession is the prayer that is for others besides you. It is the man that has the interest of God and His kingdom that will intercede for others. A prayer of intercession means that you are standing in the gap for others. The greatest prayer you can pray as a Christian is praying for others. No matter your challenge in life, if you stand in the gap and pray for others, God will lavish you with blessings because a pipe that carries water cannot be thirsty.

The Bible says that we should intercede for all God's people. This means that you should look around you and start praying for the need of others to be met. If you are in a church and you see a brother or sister in need, the first thing you should do privately is to pray for that person. Never gossip about a church member but pray for them. If you hear any unpleasant thing about a member of your church, take it up to God in prayer on their behalf. When their situation turns around, you will rejoice in your spirit and your account in heaven will be credited.

Always have a list of people to pray for. If a sister in the church is having difficulty giving birth after marriage, stand in the gap for her to be fruitful and no one in your lineage will ever be barren. You see it is spiritual ignorance to laugh at others because they don't have what you think you have. Instead of insulting them for being childless, pray for them. Do not go and tell a brother or sister in the church that you are praying for them, no. Instead, take their matter to God in your private altar and God will hear and intervene. I have birthed many testimonies this way and the testifiers don't know that I am the reason for their testimonies. The real parents of a child who was born after many years of marriage spiritually are those that prayed. You will be surprised who the true parent of a child is when we get to heaven.

HOW TO COOK PRAYER

Praying for others, especially in the church will help you to overcome gossip because you cannot be praying for someone and be gossiping about them at the same time. Apart from praying for others in church, you should also pray for the salvation of souls in your community or country depending on your spiritual jurisdiction assigned. Every born-again Christian has a spiritual jurisdiction and when you find out yours, stand in the gap and pray for the unsaved. Your prayer can go a long way to get souls saved. The reason why people get saved is not because you went out to share flyers during evangelism. The real reason why people will listen to you and follow you to church is that someone prayed somewhere. The harvest of souls is more spiritual than physical. The prayer that is prayed in the church helps, but souls are saved on the knees of intercessors on a personal altar.

The heartbeat of God, for now, is the salvation of the souls of men. God does not want people to follow the devil to hell, so He depends on your prayer for them to be saved. When you stand in the gap for souls to be saved in your territory, you have activated the ministry of angels who will go and direct the steps of the unsaved to those going out for evangelism. You have heard or seen many people come to church without being invited or preached to. This is what intercession can do.

When you intercede for the salvation of souls, the Holy Spirit will direct their steps to the church, and you will see them coming in multitudes. The reason why people go out for altar call after the sermon may not be because the minister preached a good message that touched their hearts. It may be because you prayed them into receiving Jesus and heeding the altar call is the physical manifestation of your prayer.

You should also intercede for your country because if anything is wrong in the country you live in, it will affect you. Don't live in America and pray for Ghana. You may be a Ghanian but if you live in London, that is your jurisdiction. If it goes bad in London, it will affect you. **Where you live and earn a living is your primary place of spiritual**

assignment therefore you must intercede for that territory first.

We are admonished in scripture to pray for those in authority. So, it is the will of God for you to pray for leaders in the government of your country and or state, 1 Timothy 2:2. When you intercede for your government leaders, God will help them to make the right policy that will make life wonderful for you and your family.

The reason why there are so many problems in our political system is that children of God are not praying but complaining. Complaining will not help but intercession will. I rarely see churches praying for the government instead what I see is selfish prayer. But the church fails to understand that they can only function as far as the government allows. If you don't pray for leaders in government, they may make policies that can stop your operation. Government is powerful, and you need God to touch their heart to favor the church and this can only be achieved by intercession. Although the bible says that the heart of a king is in God's hand Proverb 21:1,

He will only turn it to favor the church when the church intercedes for them.

Understand that the government cannot destroy the church, that is the eternal order, but they can make life difficult for the church. If the church doesn't pray for the government leaders, they may wake up one day and demand the church start paying taxes, and pastors should get a license before being allowed to preach. They may even demand that churches submit teaching outlines to the government for vetting before being allowed to preach. This is to avoid hate speech, they may claim. I believe these acts are in the pipeline and they can only succeed to implement if the church doesn't pray.

We should also pray for our communities. There is a rise in crime and violence and many lives have been lost. We don't know who the next victim will be but when we intercede for our communities, God will intervene. Our families need us to stand in the gap for them. We should pray for members of our family that are not yet born again or live a life that does not please God.

We should stand in the gap for our spouses, children, and in-laws even when we don't like them or agree with them. Political differences should not stop us from interceding for our family members whether close or extended. We should know that God is looking up to us to stand in the gap for others. When we intercede for others as enumerated, we would stop many negative things from happening.

Ezekiel 22:30

I searched for a man among them who would build up the wall and stand in the gap before Me for [the sake of] the land, that I would not destroy it, but I found no one [not even one]. AMP

God is looking for a man that will stand in the gap and intercede for others and if you become that intercessor, you will help to stop the destruction that was supposed to happen.

The ministry of intercession is important because it makes you a stand between God and man. Your intercession can stop the operation of darkness within your family, community, or country. Even God is looking for someone to stand between Him and a nation so that He will not destroy it. This means that if you do not intercede for your community, or family, they may be destroyed, and you will be blamed for it.

Intercession is a powerful weapon that can stop negative things from happening. It can cause a notorious criminal to repent and even cause the government to reverse evil plans that would negatively impact the lives of people.

It does not take a group to change the course of things but the knee of an intercessor.

Chapter 20

Importunity in Prayer

Luke 18:5-7

yet because this widow continues to bother me, I will give her justice and legal protection; otherwise [a]by continually coming she [will be an intolerable annoyance and she] will wear me out.' ⁶ *Then the Lord said, "Listen to what the unjust judge says!* ⁷ *And will not [our just] God defend and avenge His elect [His chosen ones] who cry out to Him day and night? Will He delay [in providing justice] on their behalf?* AMP

HOW TO COOK PRAYER

You must never give up in prayer until you receive an answer. Importunity in prayer is important because it makes God know that we have no other source except Him, and if He does not intervene there is nowhere else to go. When you keep going to God in prayer about an issue, you become like that woman in the above scripture who kept bothering the unjust judge until her request was granted. And God says if an unjust judge responded why wouldn't He the just God respond and grant your petition. Giving up in prayer concerning an issue because God did not answer shows weakness and lack of trust. You should never give up. Keep going to God and presenting that request until you get a response. It does not matter how long it takes; God will always respond to your request.

The reason why many requests experience a delay in response is that we may not have cooked it well. From this book, we have learned how to cook the right prayer and with this understanding, look at that issue again and see if the presentation was right and do it better and you may be surprised at how speedily your answer may come.

Sometimes God purposely refuses to respond to our request because that is not what we need. It may be a case is pending in the court of heaven and until that is cleared, the answer may not come. You may be asking God for a promotion at your job, but God wants you to remain at the level you are right now so that you can learn things that are needed for the top that you are looking for. It could be that the reason why your prayer for God to remove the evil boss of yours and no answer is in sight is that God wants you to learn patience and tolerance and when you pass that test, the answer will come.

A lot of time we ask God for things, but we have not built the capacity to handle what we are asking for. This can cause a delay but that doesn't mean you should stop praying. I remember that for many years I used to pray for financial breakthroughs. That was my number one and most important prayer point. But I don't think I needed a financial breakthrough at that time. What I needed was to develop myself to handle what I was praying for. One day, I was given one million Nigerian naira to do a business, and would you believe that I put that money in my pocket and could not account for what I did with it. Within a month, the money finished. Riches indeed have wings, Proverb 23:5. The money vanished from me, and I was in need again.

You see, sometimes what we pray for is not what we need. We should develop ourselves to handle what we keep praying to God about and as we keep building ourselves one day the answer will come. When we understand this, we will not stop praying about an issue but will keep going. Whatever you have laid before God in prayer, do not give up.

If you are praying for God to touch the heart of your spouse or change your wayward child, do not give up because one day, the answer will come. If you are looking for a life partner and until now no one has shown up, keep pressing and the answer will come. Don't say that I have been praying about this issue for a long time and nothing seems to happen. Keep praying because you never know if you are closer to receiving your answer or if your file has been brought before God, and if you stop praying you may miss it.

I have heard some people say that they are tired of praying for a particular person and so they give up. Some people told me when I was not married that they are tired of praying for me and so they stopped. You do not stop praying for someone simply because you have not seen the desired change or testimony. You should keep praying until you receive the answer. Some people prayed for many years for someone to repent and give their life to Jesus and because they did not give up, that soul was rescued from destruction. Never give up in prayer. No matter what the issue is, keep praying and one day the answer will come.

Chapter 21

Praying to Receive Answer

Mark11:24

For this reason I am telling you, whatever things you ask for in prayer [in accordance with God's will], believe [with confident trust] that you have received them, and they will be given to you. AMP

You should always pray to receive an answer. When you pray to God, believe that He can answer you and give you what you are requesting. It is a waste of time and energy to pray without expecting answers. Prayer is hard work, and it is a gross waste of time and energy to pray without expecting to receive an answer. It is not until we verbalize our doubt before it shows we don't expect an answer. Our actions after prayer can signify that we don't expect the answer to our request. The Bible says that when we pray, we should believe that we have received what we asked for, and when we believe we will receive. In my opinion, believing is more important because no matter how well you cook your prayer, if you don't believe, you just wasted your time.

Prayer has a lot to do with the state of our mind. When you believe you will receive and when you don't believe that your prayer will be answered, there will be no results. Confidence in God's ability to give us what we want is what draws us to prayer in the first place. It should be what produces the answer. If you think that God will not be able to give you what you want, why go to Him in the first place. God wants us to believe that He has all it takes to give us our request, and when we believe, an answer is inevitable. Children believe that when they request from their parents, they will receive an answer irrespective of the magnitude of the request. Children don't know if the parent has the money to fund their request but will go about telling their friends that their parents will buy them what they asked for. Sometimes they may even put a date on when their request should be given.

For instance, a child may request a particular toy to be given to them on their birthday without a thought if the parent can afford it. When the day draws closer, some parents will become anxious as the child will keep reminding them of the request. If we can behave like children when we make a request to God, then we will be swimming in an abundance of supplies. What children exhibit is called trust. If we trust that God will always answer us, we will have whatever we requested. Be aware that heaven does not store prayers requesting earthly things. God will not ask the angels to archive your request for a husband or breakthrough in business. When you request, it is either answered or returned based on the protocol you engaged.

Many prayers have been answered but you wonder why the supposed recipient hasn't taken delivery. What you prayed for years ago was granted but you have not received the answer because of unbelief. If you have cooked the right prayer following accurate protocol, the answer was given but unbelief may have trapped the answer and kept it in the realm of the spirit. The reason we see some Christians receiving a heavy downpour of blessings is that when understanding comes like the one you are getting from this book, they reach out to the spirit realm and claimed their hanging blessings, Proverb 13:15.

Also, the reason why many do not receive the answer to their request is that they are serving two masters. They will pray to God, but their heart is somewhere else. They will tell you they believe in God whereas they trust in a man to answer them. For instance, they can pray to God for a job, but they trust that the uncle or in-law will help them to get the job.

They prayed to God based on who they had in a position to answer their prayer. These types of people do not pray to receive an answer. They only pray for formality because their heart is not in God.

When you pray, always believe that God can and will answer you no matter what you are asking for. With this understanding, never ask God for small things. If you know who God is, you will never request bread and butter. Instead of asking God for a house, ask Him for an estate and if you follow the right protocol, you will receive it. Let me teach you something, if you want to get it big from God, always ask yourself first what is in it for God. Do you know that some people will approve your proposal if they have a percentage of the proceeds? Hannah showed us an example in 1 Samuel 1:11.

Don't wait for God to find out what He will gain from your request because you may wait for a long time. Tell God what is in it for Him from what you are asking. If you want God to open doors of contract for you, what will He gain? Will you use the money made from the contract to advance his kingdom? Or if you are requesting for car, will that car serve His purpose? Will you use that car to assist others in your neighborhood to get to church or will you use it to carry your girlfriends?

When you want to ask God for something, ask big and tell Him specifically what you want and how that thing will serve His purpose, and you will receive an answer. **Know that the storehouse of heaven is never depleted**. All that you will ever desire in this life is not needed in heaven, they were prepared for us here on the earth. If you have this understanding, you will hate poverty or scratching a living. Heaven hates it when you are poor or managing life. I hate it as well.

Let me use this opportunity to inform you that heaven is emptying its warehouse and we are in the era of wealth transfer. What will distinguish the last day's church which is you, is supernatural wealth. But unfortunately, it is few born-again Christians that will enjoy it. You are not living your full potential as a redeemed soul if you are managing life, so ask.

God wants to give you everything because Jesus paid for it, and it pains God to see His children managing life. Wealth is a mentality and poverty is first a mentality. If you have a wealth mentality, it will reflect in your life sooner or later. Some of God's children cannot spend money and buy good things for themselves even when they have the money. Many don't eat well or dress well and if you see where they live you will wonder why. Learn to ask God big things and He will do it. God is excited to give you your request so, you should expect to receive an answer when you pray.

Chapter 22

Cooking Time of Prayer

Proverb 16:1

The preparations of the heart in man, and the answer of the tongue, is from the Lord. KJV

You must prepare before you enter the prayer room. Prayer requires lots of preparation no matter what you are praying for. I gave you an analogy of my wife's preparation before cooking. This is the same way you should prepare before you engage in prayer. It does not matter what type of prayer, the urgency, or location, prayer needs to be prepared to cook right. The cooking time of prayer is the time of preparation. This is the time you put your thoughts together on what you want to pray about. This has a lot to do with mental preparation. You know what the issue is and so you think about how you will put the prayer together to make it right.

Remember that you are appearing before the Judge of the whole earth and you have an accuser who doesn't want the judge to approve your request, so you prepare what you will say. When you are done with mental preparation, then you go in search of what the will of God says concerning the issue. This is the time of digging deep. The Internet has made it easy now to harvest scriptures without having to turn the pages of the bible one by one to find out which is relevant to your need. There are bible concordance and translations that explains in footnotes on some topics, you engage in them to harvest what you want.

The time of scripture search is very important in the cooking process because you will make lots of discoveries. It may be while you are scavenging the

Bible, your need becomes a workover without you having to pray about it. We have heard this several times in testimonies. So, don't take the preparation period for granted because you may have a revelation that can turn that situation around.

After you have finished gathering relevant scriptures, it is time to put them together. Remember that when you are ready to cook, there is what you add first. Know what to put first and what follows, a mistake in adding ingredients can spoil the food. Some foods require that you start with water while others may need to fry the oil. No matter what prayer you are cooking, know what to add first and the quantity. You should know how long to fry the oil or steam the water of your prayer and the ingredient that is to be added next.

Every ingredient in cooking has a time frame, you do not put salt at the end of the cooking process or add onions when you are done. You should know what comes first in cooking your prayer and what follows.

HOW TO COOK PRAYER

As you cook your prayer, know when to stir or else your prayer will not mix well. This has to do with the name of Jesus. You begin with him, continue with him, and end with him. You also keep adding the word to mix until it is done. Remember, the best way to cook the right prayer is to put God first. When you put God as the first ingredient, your prayer will turn out right. Your need should not come first but the kingdom. The Bible says you should seek first the kingdom of God. I pray that as you cook your prayer, it will turn out right for you in Jesus' name.

Chapter 23

Prayer Spices

Galatians 5:22

But the fruit of the Spirit is love, joy, peace, longsuffering, gentleness, goodness, faith, KJV

There are things you can add to make your prayer smell nice and taste good. These are called prayer spices and they include worship, thanksgiving, love, patience, hope, and joy. Prayer like food requires certain spices to distinguish it from other food. What makes a chef unique and stand out is the ability to locate spices that make the food have a unique smell and taste. In most cases, these spices are guarded jealously, and they become a signature ingredient that makes the chef or food to be sought after. For instance, Coca-Cola has a secret ingredient that makes coke unique. This secret is well guarded and till today, no other soft drink has the unique taste of coke.

As a prayer chef, you should be aware of the prayer spices that can make your prayer stand out. Every second of the day, prayers ascend to heaven, but your prayer spices can make angels spot your prayer quickly and deliver it to God on the express lane.

WORSHIP

Praise and worship put your prayer on the express lane. You should never start prayer without first worshiping God. Worship attracts the presence of God and when God comes down, the matter is settled. It is not even right for you to start talking to God without adoring His name and worshiping His majesty. God is great and we should not appear before Him with our request without taking time to worship Him and magnify His holy name no matter how short that prayer is.

THANKSGIVING

You should always thank God for all that He has done in your life before you present any request. If you don't give thanks, your prayer will be pushed aside. A person who refuses to start a prayer with thanksgiving is expressing an ungrateful heart. Even when you think He has not done anything for you, your life alone is enough. **Is it not because you are alive that is why you can pray in the first place?** Thanksgiving shows that we appreciate God's mercy and benevolence and when you appreciate, God will answer your prayer. Thanksgiving is a spice that opens doors and the more you thank God, the more He will answer your prayer.

LOVE

Your prayer will go as far as your love for God. If God is the number one in your life, your prayer will always receive a speedy answer. Many people pray to God that is not a priority in their life. They only pray to God to give them while they have nothing to offer in return. I call these people collectors. They only want to receive all the time. To them, God is a supplier and when they can't get anything from God, they stop calling Him.

Love is very important in prayer because when you love God, you may not need to ask and when you do ask, He responds before you make an end to your request. The reason why God gave us His son to die for us is because of love. God loves man so much that He had to send His only son to die for man's sin. When we reciprocate the love of God, He will always answer our prayers.

When you stand to pray, add a little bit of love. Let what matters to God matter to you. If you love God, your prayer will always start with kingdom advancement. You will always be interested in praying first to advance His purposes. Many Christians pray a selfish prayer. They are more interested in themselves and their immediate families and forget that God has needs. When you locate the need of God and bring them first in prayer, you may not need to ask for anything and if you do, your prayer will smell so nice and taste very good.

PATIENCE

Patience is a spice that you need when you cook prayer. Without patience, your prayer food will have a sour taste and not smell nice. God is in heaven and is never in a hurry so when you pray, don't hurry God. For your prayer to be granted, you need patience. Imagine you asking the president of your country to do something for you, and you begin to hurry him or her. In fact, if you call the president about your case and he said he will look into it, you may even tell him to take his time out of respect. But when you come to God, you want it done fast. You must learn to relax and keep calm while heaven is reviewing your case. Some of the things we ask from God, we don't need and if we do, the time may not be right.

I remember when I was looking for a house and I got one, I was very excited but later lost it. I was not happy, and I asked God why he allowed me to lose the house. After some time, what God gave me was far better than the one I lost. I told my wife if I had gotten the first and later showed the one I got later, I would have cried. Patience will always get you the best. If God were to answer all your prayers immediately or as you want it, you will be in serious trouble. When you pray, be patient. While waiting, give thanks, because the king of the universe knows what you need and when you need them.

HOPE

Hope is a spice that you need when you cook prayer. Adding hope to your food will give it a good taste. When faith is lost, hope will keep going. In Romans 5:5 the Bible says, *and hope maketh not ashamed; because the love of God is shed abroad in our hearts by the Holy Ghost which is given unto us.* Hope is that thing that you believe will happen. You may think that something will not happen but then have this feeling that what you ask God will surely be given you. This shows that you have hope. Hope in God will not allow you to see shame because it is the highest form of belief. Faith may fail according to

Luke 22:32 but hope never to fail. When your faith fails, hope will keep you going.

Adding hope as a spice to your prayer meal will make the food taste delicious and no matter how long it takes the answer will surely come. Remember as you go to purchase ingredients for your prayer meal, buy hope in large quantity because it will make your prayer food smell nice and bring answers.

JOY

Joy is a vital spice in prayer food preparation. The moment you add joy to your food, even your enemies will know that you have cook something. Joy is a facilitator; it is a door opener. Joy will distinguish your prayer and angels will spot it immediately. The Bible says *therefore with joy shall ye draw water out of the wells of salvation*, Isaiah 12:3. Joy will always make your prayer be answered on time. You can only receive from God with a joyful heart. No matter what you lost in life, never lose your joy because the moment joy is gone, there will be no harvest. Joel 1:12 *The vine is dried up, and the fig tree languisheth; the pomegranate tree, the palm tree also, and the apple tree, even all the trees of the field, are withered: because joy is withered away from the sons of men.* Without joy, your prayer will be stale and even you won't eat it.

Joy is an important spice in prayer making process and you should never forget to add it. Hannah was always sorrowful even though she attended Shiloh faithfully and cooked prayer. But the day she let go of a sorrowful spirit and purchased joy, her prayer was answered immediately, 1 Samuel 1:15. Your prayer will remain in the cloud if you are not joyful. The scripture above says that when joy is absent, everything withers away. The reason why many prayers remain unanswered is that joy is lacking. Carrying long faces as if you are fighting with God will not make your prayer turn out well. When you are joyful despite what you may be going through, God will respond to you.

Therefore, to make a good prayer, add the spice of worship, thanksgiving, love, patience, hope, and joy and the aroma of your prayer will attract God to your affairs.

You know that your neighbor that when she cooks, you feel like going to her house with a plate to ask for some. That is how your prayer should smell. In my village, there are some leaves that when you add to your food, everybody will greet you and desire to eat. Despite that these leaves are there in the forest and sometimes sold in the market, not everyone knows about them or cares to get some. But when someone put them in their food, the smell attracts the entire neighborhood. Don't just cook prayer, cook the one that will smell and block the nose of your enemy but attracts angels. Your understanding of the prayer spices will become your secret ingredient in your prayer recipe.

Chapter 24

Steam of Faith

> Hebrew 11:1,6
> *Now faith is the substance of things hoped for, the evidence of things not seen. But without faith it is impossible to please him: for he that cometh to God must believe that he is, and that he is a rewarder of them that diligently seek him.* KJV

Steaming is important in cooking because it is steaming that makes all the ingredients in the food mix and turns the raw taste of the food into something edible. Without steaming, the food will not have a taste no matter the type of ingredients used. Faith is therefore the steam that makes your prayer work. When you approach God in prayer, you must have faith in Him. The Bible says it is impossible to please God without faith. A person without faith is not pleasing the lord and if you don't please God, your prayer will go nowhere.

When you cook prayer that you want God to answer, you must steam it in faith. This means that you must trust God to answer your prayer. It is faith that makes our prayer answerable. Faith is a substance of things hoped for. What you want is not in view, but you have faith that as you go to God in prayer, it will become a reality. No matter what people say or how the circumstance may look, faith will keep you focused on God. Matthew 17:20,

And Jesus said unto them, Because of your unbelief: for verily I say unto you, If ye have faith as a grain of mustard seed, ye shall say unto this mountain, Remove hence to yonder place; and it shall remove; and nothing shall be impossible unto you. KJV

It is your faith that will move the mountain. Many Christians pray fervently but only a few have faith in God. Many have cooked the right prayer with mouthwatering spices, but the lack of faith spoiled the food. Faith is an important part of the prayer-making process that makes our prayer meal delicious. Jesus emphasized more faith than actual prayer. When you have faith in God, your prayer will be quick and precise.

The reason why some engaged in long prayer is because of a lack of faith. Some churchgoers want the pastor to pray long prayers and demonstrate before they believe the prayer will work. If the pastor says a few words, they think that prayer is not going anywhere. It is not in the volume but faith. Most of the prayers that I received immediate answers were short and precise because I had faith that God will do them.

God looks at our hearts when we pray and what He looks for is our faith. If you do not have faith, don't take any steps to pray because it will be a waste of time. Faith is what should drive us to a place of prayer. In cooking prayer, steam it well with faith. Some food requires extensive steaming while others require only a few seconds on the fire. But to cook something worthwhile, the pot must be on the stove for a long time. There is food you cook on an electric stove but there are others that need firewood to produce a good meal. If you cook for a big occasion where you must serve many people, an industrial stove may be needed.

So, depending on what you are praying for, there is a degree of steaming (faith) that you must engage. May God give you understanding.

Chapter 25

The Salt of Purity

Job 22:30

He shall deliver the island of the innocent: and it is delivered by the pureness of thine hands. KJV

Luke 14:34-35

Therefore, salt is good; but if salt has become tasteless, with what will it be seasoned? ³⁵ It is fit neither for the soil nor for the manure pile; it is thrown away. He who has ears to hear, let him hear and heed My words. AMP

HOW TO COOK PRAYER

Salt is very important in the cooking process. The taste of food depends on the salt and when salt is absent, that food will never be eaten and the effort that you put in cooking the food will be wasted. Purity is the salt that you add to your prayer to give it a taste. Without purity, your prayer will be tasteless. If you are not clean, you cannot lift your face to heaven in prayer. If you try to pray to God, your conscience will condemn you and let you know that your prayer is not going anywhere. Sin blocks our prayer. The devil will mock your utterance in prayer if you are living in sin.

When you approach God in prayer or want to cook answer delivering prayer, you must first assess yourself and see if there is anything like a sin that may block your prayer. Living in sin and praying to God is an insult. It means that you are reporting yourself to heaven that you sinned. What many Christians don't know is that when they appear in a place of prayer, demons and angels are present and they all assess you to see if there is any sin in your life.

We have established the fact that the kingdom of darkness does not want you to receive anything from God so, when you approach God in prayer, they scan you for sin. When the scanner beeps, your utterance is disqualified no matter how long you stay or the degree of your tears. This is the reason why you should constantly check yourself before you pray to God.

God is holy and anyone who appears before Him must be holy. 1 Peter 1:15-16, *But as he which hath called you is holy, so be ye holy in all manner of conversation; Because it is written, Be ye holy; for I am holy.* God is holy and He cannot behold sin. If you are living in sin, you should first seek forgiveness before you present your request to God. Let your conscience be clear and your hands pure before you pray to God. Do not engage in prayer when there is sin in your life.

Many believers are frustrated today in prayer because sin blocks their access, and they blame God for not answering them. It is important to know that if you live a clean life, you will pray less. The prayer you will cook if your hands are clean will be kingdom advancement and praying for others, you will not need to ask God for anything.

God wants to bless His children, but sin has been a major hindrance. Just try and live in purity and see how your life will turn out in three months. Many times, the reason why we bombard heaven requesting things is that we don't have a right standing with God.

As you cook prayer, the only thing that will give it taste is the salt of purity and as soon as this is added, the answer will come. I will therefore admonish you to live a holy life. There is nothing out there that is better than a relationship with God. If there was something better than God in the world I would know because I was fully involved. There is nothing you call enjoyment that I did not experience but I can tell you now, that a relationship with God is better. You are not suffering if you leave the world and stay with God. Going to church, praying, and reading the bible is not boring but advancement. I am more at peace now than when I was carrying women, drinking, and smoking. It looks funny to me now when I see people think that they are enjoying doing the things of the world.

When I was in the world, I thought I was having fun until I met Jesus and my perspective changed. You cannot claim to be a Christian and be living in sin, in fact, you are worse than an unbeliever. Do not crucify Jesus a second time by going back to your vomit, repent and ask God for forgiveness in earnest so that you can cook the prayer that has taste. If you are not pure, your prayer is tasteless, and angels will throw it out and march it on foot. You wouldn't want your effort to be thrown out so live holy.

As a born-again Christian, your life is on a narrow path. You do not have the luxury of living like the unsaved. Matthew 7:13,

Enter ye in at the strait gate: for wide is the gate, and broad is the way, that leadeth to destruction, and many there be which go in thereat: KJV

A believer should not compromise in any way. You must be careful how you live and the things you do. The narrow path means there are things you should not do or be involved. The reason why unbelievers don't want to give their lives to Jesus is that they don't want to stop doing what they call fun. They know that giving their lives to Jesus means strict compliance with biblical doctrine. If you are a believer and still live like those in the world, you are in a broad way. If you don't retrace your steps, it will lead you to the same place sinners will end. I wish I could make it sound nice, but that is the raw truth.

Purity will give your prayer taste; it will help you to prepare a good meal that you and others will enjoy eating. A prayer that comes from a pure heart will always attract God's attention. Demons will not be able to contest a prayer that comes from a clean heart. You may say that you are not living in sin but how is your conversation? What are the things that come out of your mouth? You cannot claim to be a born-again child of God and be using curse words and lewd words that do not glorify God. That is sin.

Giving your house to your friends to sleep with their girlfriend or boyfriend when they are not married is a sin even if you don't do that yourself. Cheering someone who is a pro in sleeping around or committing fraud is a sin and must be repented of.

Masturbation and watching pornography are serious sins and must be repented of. Some born-again believers are addicted to masturbation and some Christian sisters have sex toys at home. Some think that because they are not sleeping with a man, they are holy, no. Using a tool to please yourself sexually is sinful. Some born-again believers may not do the act but encourage or applaud those who do them.

Doing yoga and deep meditation is a sin. You should only meditate on the word of God. Engaging in tarot cards, zodiac signs, and palm reading is a sin. Celebrating Halloween, going to the club, and engaging in wild partying is sinful.

Making friends with people that defraud the government or applaud the act is a sin. If you stole public funds to enrich yourself is a sin, and now that you are born again, you must restitute by returning the looted funds.

Lying is a sin and there is no white or black lie, a lie is a lie. You must be truthful always as a child of God. Do not be involved in fraud. Love and respect your spouse and be sincere one with another. Many spouses live a lie. They keep things from each other but pretend to be perfect and holy. You must be clean inside out for your prayer to be answered.

Now, you may see why many prayers are not answered and this revelation should make you carry out self-appraisal before you begin to cook your prayer. Purity is the salt that will give your prayer taste, add it in the required quantity.

Chapter 26

Ingredient of Righteousness

2 Corinthians 5:21

For he hath made him to be sin for us, who knew no sin; that we might be made the righteousness of God in him. KJV

1 Corinthians 6:20

For ye are bought with a price: therefore glorify God in your body, and in your spirit, which are God's. KJV

HOW TO COOK PRAYER

The number one ingredient you must have to cook prayer is righteousness. This righteousness is not what you achieve on your own, it is what was done for you. You must be purchased by the blood else you cannot cook the prayer that will smell nice, have taste, and reach God. The prayer of the unrighteous stinks before God. Hear this, *God judgeth the righteous, and God is angry with the wicked every day, Psalm 7:11*. The wicked here is someone that is not born again. Anyone who is not born again does not please God in any way no matter what they do. Even if you were born in the church, you must give your life to Jesus to be accepted. Until you surrender to Jesus and accept him as your lord and savior, you are not righteous.

The only prayer a sinner can pray, and God will listen, and answer, is a prayer of repentance. If you are not born again, God will not hear your prayer, it does not matter how you pray or what anyone told you.

To cook answer delivering prayer, the ingredient of righteousness is required. Jesus died and paid the price for your sin and to be righteous, you must accept him. The punishment that should have come upon us because of the sin of our first parent was put upon him and when you accept him, you automatically become righteous. Is that not great? Someone paid the price for you already; all you must do is accept his sacrifice and you will become righteous.

Let me tell you why you need to accept Jesus as your lord and savior and be born again. Man is a contaminated product, and you know what happens when a manufacturer creates a product, and that product becomes contaminated. It is thrown out or destroyed. God created man perfect, but the devil came and contaminated man, and made him sin against God. Since man became a contaminated product, he is only fit for destruction. But God in His mercy decided to make a way for man to be recreated without being destroyed. This He did by sending His only son to come and die for man. Anyone who accepts His son will not be destroyed but will be redeemed. This is called new birth or new creation or born again. Those who refused will be thrown out and destroyed.

Man is a spirit and spirits don't die. The only way to destroy this contaminated product called man is by fire. The fire for destruction was created for the devil, to be punished for his sin of rebellion. And since there is no place for a man to be destroyed, God decided to put the man in the same place he prepared for Satan and his angels who sinned against Him. This place is called hell.

When you accept Jesus as lord and savior, you become a new creation and designated righteous. It is this righteousness that gives you a right or legal standing before the Father; this is when your prayer can reach heaven and be answered.

The ingredient of righteousness is what will make your prayer have access to heaven. If you pray without having the right standing with God through the blood of His son Jesus, your prayer is a waste. It doesn't matter what you used in cooking your prayer.

There are many churchgoers who are not born again, and they think that being in the church has given them access to make a prayer. **Having a big ecclesiastical title does not translate to righteousness, you must be born again.** If you are not born again, you are not righteous and when you are not righteous, you cannot cook answer delivering prayer.

Righteousness is the ingredient that you cannot do without in cooking prayer. If you do not have the righteousness of God, that prayer food must be kept from cooking until it is purchased. The good news is that provision has been made for you to accept Jesus as your lord and personal savior in our preceding chapter. When you sincerely pray that prayer, you become born again and the ingredient of righteousness becomes available for you to add to your prayer meal.

The scripture above says that we become the righteousness of God because someone was made a sin for us, and that person is Jesus. You cannot make yourself righteous, and you certainly cannot pay for your sin. Someone without sin had to pay for you to become righteous and your only job is to accept the sacrifice that he made.

Proverb 14:34

Righteousness exalteth a nation:
but sin is a reproach to any people. KJV

Being born again will make you righteous before God. It is this righteousness, that will exalt you and bring you close to God. Sin is a reproach. You cannot get close to God as an unsaved soul, and you cannot stand before Him in prayer except for a prayer of repentance.

We have been bought by the blood of Jesus that is why we have the right standing with God and can lift our faces to Him in prayer. When you become born again, you are righteous and accepted into the family of God. Your prayer as a redeemed soul will smell nice and ascend to heaven without hindrance.

Chapter 27

Adding Fasting to Prayer

Matthew 17:21,
Howbeit this kind goeth not out but by prayer and fasting. KJV

Esther 4:16
Go, gather together all the Jews that are present in Shushan, and fast ye for me, and neither eat nor drink three days, night or day: I also and my maidens will fast likewise; and so will I go in unto the king, which is not according to the law: and if I perish, I perish. KJV

HOW TO COOK PRAYER

Jonah 3:5

So the people of Nineveh believed God, and proclaimed a fast, and put on sackcloth, from the greatest of them even to the least of them. KJV

Fasting expedites our prayer. it is a booster that makes the answer to our prayer come fast. When the issue persists, you should add fasting. Fasting is like adding limestone to food that takes a long time to cook. In my country, while growing up, our neighbors used to add limestone to make their beans or meat cook fast. My mom did not like limestone, so we took a long time to cook. By the time our food is done, others had finished eating. Adding fasting to prayer is like adding limestone, it helps to make it cook faster.

There are some issues or challenges that will not go away until you add fasting to the prayer. There are stubborn issues that adding fasting can help to overcome. Esther knew this so she added fasting to her prayer and when she appeared, the king gave her an audience.

Instead of sitting and waiting for the answer to your prayer, why not add fasting. Fasting is a big booster and can bring your answer fast. Remember Jesus says in Matthew 17:21, *Howbeit this kind goeth not out but by prayer and fasting.* There are certain things that we pray for that may not be answered unless we add fasting. There are *these kinds* that adding fasting can deal with. If you want quick results, add fasting to your prayer. The more you add fasting to your prayer, the more results you get. Prayer alone in many cases may not have power and until fasting is introduced, you may remain in one spot.

As a child of God, you should make fasting a part of your life. Many Pentecostal churches have a tradition of fasting on the first month of the year. I have observed over the years that some Christians do not like to attend church during this period because of fasting. If you claim to be a child of God and you don't like to fast, you certainly need to rethink your

Christian walk. It is important to fast else prayer will become a burden. Sometimes you can decide to stay away from food to fine-tune your spiritual antenna.

If you don't fast, you may not intermeddle with spiritual things. Understand that it is not only born-again Christians that fast, evil people do fast also. The people from other religions which you know have a season of fasting which they carry out with pomp and pageantry. If the people who are not born again fast and pray why shouldn't you. **If you want to go far spiritually, you should fast often.**

Fasting is good for your health which is physical and spiritual health. No matter how prayerful you think you are, if you don't fast, you will not increase spiritually. The occultic people fast regularly and one even confessed that when they want to bring down a church or a strong man of God, they fast. If the devil prescribes fasting for his followers, why wouldn't a child of God give his or herself to fasting?

Fasting when combined with prayer is an atomic bomb and will result in speedy answers. Jesus told the Pharisees that a time will come when his disciple will fast, Matthew 9:15. He was saying that the disciple will not be able to escape fasting so allow them to have fun now but when I leave, they will have no choice but to fast.

For you to receive anything tangible from God, you must give yourself to fasting. Fasting makes your prayer ascend to the throne of grace fast and no demon can stand to frustrate your prayer when fasting is involved. When you fast as a child of God, you are putting your flesh under your control. The flesh wants to eat, drink, and have fun but fasting starves the flesh of fun.

If you want to stop addiction, lust, and filthiness in your life, fasting is the way to go. Try it and see, after three days of fasting without breaking, you will notice that interest in things you were addicted to will vanish. Fasting will cure you of any ailment no matter what it was. If you want that stubborn sickness or disease to go, do not bother your pastor again for prayer, take to fasting.

Fasting can eradicate any unwanted issue or challenge in your life. When you fast, you allow God to purge you spiritually and physically. It has been proven medically that fasting helps to clean the body of toxins, and the body can heal itself during a protracted fast. If the body can heal itself during fasting, what do you think will happen spiritually. Fasting is so powerful when carried out with fervent prayer, and Bible study.

Fasting alone without prayer is powerful and when prayer is involved, it turns into atomic or nuclear power. You can never understand the hurricane power of fasting and prayer until you engage, and the result will be devastating to the kingdom of darkness.

The reason why many Christians don't fast is that they don't understand what power lies in fasting and prayer. Fasting makes you humble yourself and when you humble yourself before God, He will elevate you. If you know the power of fasting coupled with prayer, you will never ask anyone to pray for you because that is the powerhouse of answer prayer. The day I discovered the power of fasting, I screamed because I just discovered the highway to a breakthrough in life.

A born-again Christian who lives a fasted life will become victorious in all areas of life. I knew that I will never be trampled anymore by the devil through fasting discovery. It was one of the best discoveries of my life. Fasting will never be a burden when you make this discovery yourself. Before now, I hated to fast, when fasting was announced in church, I did not like it. I dreaded January because for three weeks I would be tormented and can't wait for the fasting to end. But when I discovered that fasting was my express road to breakthrough, I couldn't wait for January to come.

Apart from church-organized fasting, I have my personal fasting calendar. I can now organize twenty-one days of dry fasting and prayer for myself, and I do this two times a year. I also fast on the first of every month and three days a week for the whole year. I do this without stress. You can take days to fast on your own without blowing the trumpet. Fasting keeps me in perfect shape spiritually and physically. I will not give you any rules of fasting here but will only show you how I live and if you want to follow them, it can work for you.

When I fast, I fast. Fasting means abstaining from food, so when I fast, I abstain from food and drink only water. In my house, we eat well, and my wife cooks but when I declare my personal fasting, I do not impose it on my family. They can eat. In fact, I help in preparing the food, but none will enter my mouth until I finish my fast. You don't have to run away from the kitchen or make unpleasant rules in your house simply because you are fasting. Anyone that wants to eat should go ahead unless it is the general church fasting which everyone should be encouraged to be a part of. If your wife is pregnant or breastfeeding, she should not be a part of the fasting and children are not to be involved. If you have young adults or older children, you should enlighten them on the importance of fasting and encourage and guide them.

Sometimes and in most cases, you the man should carry all the spiritual burden in your family when others are not able. It is you that will determine the trajectory of your family through your altar as we learned in the preceding chapters. It is important to fast completely and only drink water all through the duration of your fast. This is the real fasting. When you break your fast with food daily, that is not complete fasting, it is partial fasting. Some people eat only once a day and in the evening. If you break your fasting with food at night, what is the difference between you and the person who did not fast but eats only at night? If you want to maximize the blessedness of fasting, do it completely.

Do not engage in twenty-one-day dry fasting and prayer if you have never tried one day dry fasting. I started with three days dry and graduated to seven days drinking only water. Later I engaged in twenty-one days dry, and they all feel the same to me. Partial fasting will still produce results, but that result can never be compared to complete dry fasting. Fasting is powerful if you do it right.

As soon as you give yourself to fasting and prayer, the gates of hell will be in disarray that is when many arrows will begin to be projected against you. You will notice this as your dream pattern will change. You will also have many distractions and attacks, do not give up as this is from the kingdom of darkness trying to stop you. I remember when I started fasting before I got married, on one of my four days of dry fasting, a girl I used to admire and tried everything to get but couldn't, suddenly appeared from nowhere and texted me that she wants to sleep with me. My body started misbehaving and I almost started thinking of seeing her. I believe the Holy Spirit stepped in and help me to understand that it is an attack from hell trying to stop me from what I was doing.

When you fast, many such attacks will come and if you overcome them, you will increase in spiritual ranking. I said earlier that fasting when added with prayer produces a spiritual hurricane that can destroy the camp of the enemy. Fasting is a powerful weapon that can destroy anything on the path of the believer. Engaging in fasting and prayer is like dropping the atomic bomb, nothing can stand in its way. If you want to get rid of your enemy, add fasting to your prayer and you will see what will happen. If you are reading this book and there is an issue in your life that has defied everything, add fasting to your prayer and that issue will no longer exist.

Do you know that fasting can even change the mind of God concerning you? In 1 Kings 21:27 and 29, King Ahab humbled himself before God in fasting and God changed His mind concerning the punishment, He wanted to give Ahab. If the almighty God can change His mind because an evil king fasted, then fasting can make anything happen for you.

When you fast as we already established, you are humbling yourself before God, Psalm 69:10. When you humble yourself before God, He will hear you. Fasting is a powerful weapon, use it. There is nothing as powerful as a combination of fasting and prayer. If the kingdom of darkness and those who don't serve God engage in fasting, you should take fasting seriously. Fasting should not scare you but make you seize the opportunity to destroy your enemy.

Jesus told his disciple that this kind will never go unless fasting is added to prayer. There are stubborn evil spirits that will never go unless fasting is added to prayer. When you fast, the demon controlling your neighborhood will be aware, and you will burn an unquenchable fire in the realm of the spirit. That is why some people will not greet you again or you will have attacks in your dream that was not there before. If you want an instant judgment against your enemies, engage in fasting and prayer. If someone is troubling you and you don't know what else to do, do fasting and prayer and things will change.

Let fasting be your weapon of first choice and give no place to the enemy to flourish around you. Use fasting to dominate your territory and you will become a terror to the kingdom of darkness. God has placed this powerful weapon at our disposal, and we are not to run away but use it. When you fast, learn to pray more at night. We will deal with night prayer in the succeeding chapter but let me hint here that night prayer is more important than any other time of prayer. The night is the most spiritual time, and the highest demonic activities happen at night.

It is at night that the day is determined. That is why any Christian who doesn't pray at night might become a victim during the day. When you fast and wake up every night to pray, you will cause a lot of disaster in the kingdom of darkness and depending on how you pray and the type of prayer, your breakthrough will come like rain.

I will encourage you that no matter what you are facing in life, learn to fast and pray at night and you will emerge victorious. Life is spiritual and only those who engage in fasting and prayer live an overcomer's life. Prayer is powerful and can reroute evil arsenal against you and your destiny but at the instance of fasting, your enemies will surrender, and the war will be over.

When my wife was pregnant with our first child, I engaged in a series of fasting and prayer. Unknown to me that she was about to give birth that month, I went into twenty-one days of dry fasting and prayer.

My wife gave birth safely despite all the attacks that we had. I believe it was my fasting that God used to deliver my wife and the baby.

As a man, learn to fast and pray for your family. This world is very wicked, you do not know who your neighbor is or who that person you call a friend or family member is. If God were to open your eyes to see who people truly are, you will be afraid to go out of your house. Fortify yourself with fasting and prayer, and when you do this, you will become healthy physically, and spiritually.

The reason why families live and die in poverty is that no one in that family has taken responsibility to humble themselves in fasting and prayer on behalf of the family, and so the devil uses them as carpet. Do not allow the enemy to succeed over you and your family, take responsibility and you will be happy you did. I am enjoying life now because I paid the required price to secure that enjoyment. I pray every day that God should give me the grace to continue to pay the price for my family to keep enjoying.

The kingdom of darkness if they have their way would keep every child of God as beggars but fasting and prayer will make their wishes not come to pass over you. The people of Nineveh heard the news of impending destruction and quickly went into fasting. Their own was so serious that even babies and animals were involved. By the time they were done, God changed His mind. If a pagan nation that did not know God can proclaim a fast to avert destruction, how about you. I don't think your situation will warrant you starving your baby or animal. You should consider going on a fast when you want a breakthrough, and you will come out smiling.

Isaiah 58:6

Is not this the fast that I have chosen? to loose the bands of wickedness, to undo the heavy burdens, and to let the oppressed go free, and that ye break every yoke? KJV

God Instituted fasting. He wants His children to fast the right way. When you fast, you should use the opportunity to forgive people. This will make your fasting potent. Fasting and still harboring unforgiveness and grudges can open you to demonic attacks. Some get destroyed because they went into fasting with sin in their lives. A time of fasting is a time of repentance and forgiveness. You don't fast and still oppress people.

God says that when you fast, you must let go of everything that can keep you from maximizing the blessedness of fasting. The above scripture means that you should stop putting a burden on people, and what you cannot do, do not ask others to do it. Don't treat people badly, pay those who work for you the correct wage, and stop looking for unnecessary gain. Be truthful and nice, and contented. Fasting is a powerful spiritual exercise; you must be careful how you do it. This is what will make your fasting work.

I pray that God should open your eyes to see the power that can be generated through the mystery of fasting and prayer. And I also pray for the grace to fast and pray effectively in Jesus' name.

Chapter 28

The Cooking Pot of Prayer

2 Timothy 2:21
If a man therefore purge himself from these, he shall be a vessel unto honour, sanctified, and meet for the master's use, and prepared unto every good work. KJV

The vessel or pot where the prayer will be cooked should be clean and remain clean. You should purge yourself from every filthiness of the flesh before you start cooking prayer.

If the pot where the pray will be cooked is not clean, the food will not be good but contaminated. Imagine if you use a pot that was used in cooking food a month ago without being washed to cook another food, no one will eat that food because that pot will smell. A filthy vessel will smell in God's nose therefore ensure that your vessel is clean. God wants us to cook the right prayer and no matter how good your ingredients are or how well selected, if the pot is dirty God will not accept it.

The scripture above says that if you purge yourself from every filthiness of the flesh, your pot which is you will become a vessel unto honor and fit to cook prayer. Do not come back from your boyfriend or girlfriend's house and say God please forgive and then jump into cooking prayer. Many people are fond of sinning only to ask God to forgive them, and the next day they are back to committing the same sin. If you live like that, your pot will not be clean, it will be a vessel unto dishonor. Do not wash your pot today and tomorrow it is dirty again. The pot that must cook answer delivering prayer must remain clean always. Soiling your pot in sin and asking for forgiveness will make you detestable to God.

Remember that God is holy therefore the vessel that approaches God must be holy. **If there are stains in your pot, you should engage the scrubbing power of the blood of Jesus for thorough cleaning.** Some sins will not just go away because you ask God to forgive you, you must engage the blood of Jesus in a sincere heart cry before they go away. The sin of immorality and murder involves blood and unless the blood of Jesus is applied, they will not go away. When you commit an abortion, you have killed an innocent soul and shed innocent blood, you must cry to God and plead for mercy using the blood of Jesus. If your cry is from your heart, God will hear you and you should not go back to that sin. God will indeed forgive you of every sin, but you must ask for forgiveness from a sincere heart.

A casual prayer of forgiveness you pray on Sunday morning because of the preaching of your pastor will not be heard. This is why many calamities befall some Christians and they don't know why. Many walk about with loads of sin and are not aware. If you committed abortion and now you are married and cannot give birth, you should seek mercy first before you ask for a child. Do not think that because you are born again now and have said the sinner's prayer, heaven has forgotten what you did. When the blood of a human being is shed, the earth bears witness to that blood and the voice of that blood cries out for vengeance daily, Genesis 4:10, *and he said, What hast thou done? the voice of thy brother's blood crieth unto me from the ground.* As long as the blood keeps crying, you may not be able to get pregnant.

Life is more spiritual than physical. The reason why there are so many women who got married without being able to get pregnant could be there is a voice of blood crying against them. Sometimes it might not be caused by them but by their parent. You know yourself and if your hands are clean, speak to your parent if they did something or know the family history so that proper prayer of mercy can be engaged.

The pot that you use in cooking your prayer must always remain clean. You should not go ahead to cook prayer when the vessel is not washed. God wants you to remain clean so that you can become a vessel unto honor and fit for use. Keep your cooking pot clean and stay away from every form of filthiness. Even when you think you are not living in sin, check yourself for pride, malice, hatred, grudges, anger, lust, and lies. Check your thoughts. The things that you think do not matter may be the same thing that can defile your pot. Don't cook prayer with an unwashed pot. Remove every stain of the past food and wash it with the blood of Jesus and you will be clean to cook the right prayer.

CHAPTER 29

AVOID DOUBT

James 1:6

But he must ask [for wisdom] in faith, without doubting [God's willingness to help], for the one who doubts is like a billowing surge of the sea that is blown about and tossed by the wind. AMP

Doubt will make total nonsense of your prayer. God compares a believer who doubts to a piece of paper that the wind carries about. God hates those who doubt and when you doubt, you limit Him. God wants us to believe

Him. The angel told Mary, blessed is he that believes, and Jesus told Thomas, blessed is he who does not see yet believes, John 20:29. Doubt will make all your effort in preparing answer delivering prayer a waste. After you have gathered the right ingredients and spent time cooking, a simple thing like doubt will waste the effort and spoil the food. When you doubt in prayer, you show that God cannot answer you. A person who doubts God can only help to attract the wrath of God into their lives. I would that you don't pray than to pray and doubt.

Doubt is the opposite of faith, and without faith, it is impossible to please God. There are many Christians who trust their uncles more than God. They believe that they can get whatever they want because they have someone who is financially capable or is well placed or connected in society. They believe that the name of their father or in-law can open a door for them and so when they pray, they don't believe in the prayer. Many believe that God has a history of disappointing people, so they doubt Him in prayer. God has never disappointed any man; He is always looking to bless and prosper His children, but doubt has been a major hindrance to prayer.

When you pray, God looks at the heart more than what you say with your mouth. There were times that I prayed but I already figured out what to do. That type of prayer will never cross the roof of a house. Our heart plays a major role in prayer. We can say one thing with our mouth, but our heart is speaking a different language. The reason why many go from church to a warlock or native doctor for help is that they think God will delay or may not answer them.

There were times that when I bring an issue before God, something inside me would say that God will not answer me or that issue is not the type of thing He attends to. I did not know at the time that it was a demon that was whispering that nonsense in my ears. Sometimes I would verbalize it by saying that God will not heal me of that or will not grant me that request. This continued for a long time and the kingdom of darkness was having a party over my life until understanding came and it stopped. There is nothing I don't believe God cannot do. I trust God to do everything for me if only I can think it or say it. This has brought me into a dimension of blessing that makes me a wonder to myself.

When you doubt God, you limit Him in your life. Psalm 78:41 *Yea, they turned back and tempted God, and limited the Holy One of Israel.* When you limit God, He cannot do much for you. The king of heaven has the capacity and the capability to do more than you can ever ask or think. There is no human that can match God in doing things for you. Do not allow doubt to rob you of the blessings that God has for you. A simple faith in God can open impossible doors for you, therefore, believe that when you pray, God will answer.

Doubt is from the devil and if you give it a space, it will destroy you, your family, and your destiny. Do not doubt God, believe that He can answer your prayer and do anything if you will only ask. The scripture that says ask and it shall be given is true. If you ask, you will certainly be given and when you are given your request, you will trust God the more. Don't allow the devil to trick you into doubting God for a second. Don't be like a piece of paper that the devil will toss about. Be resolute, stand firm, and trust in God, and He will give you the desires of your heart.

If you can pray, God will answer, trust in Him. Do not doubt.

Chapter 30

Night Prayer

Acts 16:25-26

And at midnight Paul and Silas prayed, and sang praises unto God: and the prisoners heard them. And suddenly there was a great earthquake, so that the foundations of the prison were shaken: and immediately all the doors were opened, and every one's bands were loosed. KJV

There is a big difference between praying at night and praying during the day. Night prayer is more powerful than day prayer.

Everything that happens during the day was programmed or determined at night. At night, the powers of heaven are released, and demonic activities take place more during the night than the day. If you want to know, try praying at night and see the difference. Night prayer is very important because you will be involved in spiritual warfare even when you were not praying warfare prayer.

The reason why many Christians are buffeted by the devil is that they sleep too much. If you want to take back control of your life and destiny from the devil, engage in night prayer. It was at midnight that Paul and Silas prayed and sang, and heaven came down into the prison. Their release was secured and the man who slept that night almost killed himself because he was not aware that nighttime is a period of warfare.

I have the habit of waking up at night to pray and it has brought me breakthroughs. I come from a family where no one succeeds. If you tried and raise your head, they will bring you down to the lowest level and all you will do is tell stories of the good old days. If not for night prayers, I would have been like my drunk uncles that have been reduced to nothing. The night is when everything happens spiritually. Witches and warlocks use the night season to perform their operations and witch doctors and juju priest carry out their heinous acts at night.

Why is it that many sleep and wake up to experience what took place in their dream? Many people dreamt how someone inflicted a wound on them and when they woke up, they see the actual wound on them? Why do some people see themselves eating in the dream and when they wake up, they fail the exam, or interview, or the contract they thought they won is canceled? Have you ever asked yourself these questions? Why is it that what you see in the dream at night normally happens especially the bad ones?

The night is when the operation of darkness takes place and if you want to exempt yourself and your family then you must put sleep away from your eyes for some hours. If you want to succeed in life, you should wake up every night and register your voice in the realm of the spirit for at least one hour. If you do this, you will experience a change in your life.

Not everybody sleeps at night and not everyone you see spends the night on this earth. Politicians have their meetings at night and by the time you wake up as a born-again Christian, they have made the decision that will affect your life. **Every happening of the day was programmed in the night**. Know this and take it seriously. If you don't take responsibility and change the course of things at night, your day will be determined for you.

In the book of Job, God asked Job a very important question that should open your eyes to this reality. Job 38:12-13,

> *Hast thou commanded the morning since thy days; and caused the dayspring to know his place;*
> *That it might take hold of the ends of the earth,*
> *that the wicked might be shaken out of it?* KJV

The question should make you understand that you can actually command the morning, but you can only command the morning at night. What commanding the morning means is that you should order the day you are about to enter at night. So, you wake up at night and order your day and when you order your day or give a command to the morning, your day will go well, and the forces of darkness will not be able to interfere.

The morning can truly be commanded. I mentioned in the preceding chapter that everything God created has ears and when you speak, they listen. This is the reason why those who speak negative things about themselves, and their family never turn out well notwithstanding what they think they achieved. Everything has ears both living and non-living and when you give them order, they obey.

You can command your day at night to work for you and they will listen. You can give order to the sun, moon, and stars and they will work for you. **Nothing just happens, they are made to happen.** Never assume that your prosperous friend or neighbor just rises or becomes successful by luck. They may never tell you what they do but if you think it is luck then you have been deceived. Everybody uses something and if you want to fly high in life, the nighttime is when you can make that happen. There are those who fly to foreign countries at night without an airplane ticket, and when they return, they have the kind of intelligence that the government of their country cannot get. They know what is about to happen and they prepare themselves for it. Some knew about COVID-19 before it happened.

You will remain in spiritual ignorance despite your Ph.D. if you don't engage the intelligence of the spirit. Education is complete rubbish in the realm of the spirit, and a boy of ten years old can make total nonsense of a professor in this world. Life is spiritual. If you buy into this truth, you will wake up and pray. I know it is not easy but if something is pursuing you, you will certainly have to run. If you know that your family has been under affliction, why not wake up and take matters into your hand and rescue them. This is the secret of every successful individual.

When you wake up at night to pray, you will observe that the atmosphere is different. The heaven over you might be heavy and sometimes it seems that your prayer is not going anywhere. Sometimes you may feel that there is a presence in your house or that someone is looking at you. What you are experiencing is true and sometimes you might have goosebumps and you wonder why. If you are in a territory where demonic activity is heavy, you might begin to hear some strange sounds and things moving. What you do is cover yourself and your family with the blood of Jesus and continue. The best prayer at this moment is praying in the spirit and when you engage the spirit, the atmosphere will be cleared.

The devil and his agents do not want you to pray at night and so they fire arrows of sleep at believers who attempt to pray. This is why many sleep on their knees only to wake up and say the grace. If you understand the operations of darkness, you will stand on your feet and pray. When you do this consistently, you will create a hub and angelic activities will take place in your house; and the day you oversleep, they will wake you up to pray. When God asked Job if he ever commanded the morning, He told him what that command will do. God says that commanding your morning will cause the dayspring to know his place and the wicked will be shaken out of it.

When you wake up to pray at night, you will paralyze the activity of evil over your life and family, and every evil the enemy planted in your life will be uprooted. You can tell the day how you want it to go for you. You can give a command to the ordinances of heaven, and they will align themselves to work for you. This is how I live. I may not order my morning every night in English, but I know that when I pray in the spirit, my day is programmed. I also know that the command that I gave to the sun, moon, and stars and the entire constellation to work for me throughout the year still stands. So, when I don't issue a command every day, wisdom has made me program them for the whole year.

The kingdom of darkness does not play, and you too should not play. If they see a way, they will destroy every believer, but you must not allow them. When Paul and Silas prayed at night something happened and if they had slept, they would have been killed. Let me ask you, why did the angel set Peter free at night and not the day in Acts 12:7? The night is when everything happens. When you pray at night, the kingdom of darkness will not be able to stop you from accessing what God has for you. It is at night that the destinies of men are stolen and sold in the astral market. It is at night that policies formulated in the spirit realms are handed over to men, and they wake up to implement these policies that affect all lives within that territory.

It is at night that demonic hierarchies meet to determine the destiny of nations with the leaders of those nations in attendance. It is at night that chief executives of conglomerates go for a meeting with spirits and the agenda of these spirits is delivered, which they return in the morning to implement. Very soon, we will see wickedness on a greater scale that will make people not feel safe anymore.

The devil has a terrible agenda for this world and if you don't wake up to pray, you will fall a victim. Night prayer will keep your territory sanitized of evil and if every born-again Christian takes responsibility, we will get rid of the enemy completely.

To wake up at night to pray is not an easy task but a great sacrifice and the benefit is great. I often said that **if you are not known in the realm of the spirit, you are not important irrespective of how famous you might be on the earth.** There are those who make a mark in the spirit world and there are those who make noise on the earth. Which one are you? You should let your voice be heard in the spirit world that when they hear you, they run into hiding. Some people are threats to the demonic world that when they move to any territory, demons congregate in fear or run away.

Praying at night is the only way you can effectively control your territory and determine what happens there spiritually. **You can decree a no-fly zone in your territory and if any witch tries to fly over, they drop.** This has been a reality in many places and many witchcraft activities have been stopped because someone decides to pray at night. The reason why you may still suffer affliction is that you are not doing what you are supposed to do. Until you wake up and take control, your life and destiny will be in another person's hand.

When I pray at night, I would go about my day with joy and peace even if I don't have the time to pray during the day; but the night I don't pray, I am not always happy. I feel comfortable going about my affair during the day if I prayed at night.

Night prayer is very important, and it is the only way you can program what happens during the day. If you want victories in the battles of life, wage war during the night. If you want demons to be afraid of you, take the battle to their gates at night and as you do, they will stay clear of your territory and family.

Understand that a Christian who prays at night is a wise Christian and the more you pray the more you become a threat to the operation of darkness. The destiny of your nation and family is in your hand and the earlier you engage in night prayer the better for you and your country. While they plan evil for your country, you can counter their plan at the same time they are planning.

The devil knows how to program diabolical rulers to take political office so that they can serve his purpose but when you stand at night to engage heaven, you can determine what happens in your country. Elections are not won through votes as many thinks, but every leader of a country is selected in the realm of the spirit at night, and your vote does not matter. Your vote and voice can only matter in the politics of your country if you pray at night.

You can scatter evil gathering of darkness if you take the night seriously. You can stop the shedding of innocent blood in your community or territory if you stand upon your watch at night. If Christians know the value of night prayer and engage, they will take over the affairs of this world.

Therefore, maximize the night season, **command the day during the night and shake every wickedness out of your heaven. Speak to the ordinance of heaven to work for you and your family and you will be free of oppression. Tell the constellation what you want and how you want the year to go. Reprogram evil done in your lineage and break evil altars raised against you and your family in the vicinity of the moon and stars. Tell the sun to burn out wickedness in your heaven and command the wind to blow away every dark cloud that demons have rolled over you. Tell the earth to reject every wickedness planted against you and the body of waters to vomit and dismantle altars erected against you. Tell the day what you want and program favor in the ordinances of heaven and your life will never remain the same.**

Make use of this knowledge that you have now, and every agent of the devil will be afraid of you. Don't keep silent anymore at night. Let the devil know that you are now wise. Wake up every night to engage in prayer and don't be afraid of whatever you experience, it is proof that you are doing the right thing. The Bible says in Psalm 74:20, *have respect unto the covenant: for the dark places of the earth are full of the habitations of cruelty.* This world is wicked, and the night is when most of the atrocities are committed.

CONTENDING WITH SPIRITUAL FORCES OF DARKNESS

Deuteronomy 2:24. *Rise ye up, take your journey, and pass over the river Arnon: behold, I have given into thine hand Sihon the Amorite, king of Heshbon, and his land: begin to possess it, and contend with him in battle.* KJV

When you wake up at night to pray, you are contending with spiritual forces of darkness. God has given us everything we need to enjoy this life, but we can only possess our possession if we contend with the enemy. The scripture above says we should begin to take possession by contending with the one that is sitting in our possession. The devil has stolen many things from God's children and instead of sitting down to cry and wail, we must contend. You will never appropriate the blessings of God if you don't contend with the spiritual forces of darkness. Witches steal destinies and blessings and keep them in the spirit realm, and you walk about here empty. There are many born-again Christians who would have become great in life, but their blessing was stolen and until they contend, they might never recover them.

The children of Israel were given the land to possess but they could not enter until they contended with those who were occupying their place. The enemy might be occupying your marriage, health, finances, joy, peace, or the fruit of the womb and until you contend, you might not get them.

I pray that as you engage in night prayer, everything that was stolen from you will be recovered. As you contend with spiritual forces of darkness in prayer, God will send His angels to take back all that is yours and you will begin to enjoy life to the fullest in the mighty name of Jesus.

Chapter 31

Wrestling With Your Angel

Genesis 32:24
And Jacob was left alone; and there wrestled a man with him until the breaking of the day. KJV

You should learn to separate yourself from people and be left alone so you can wrestle with your angel. If you are not left alone, you may never have the opportunity to interact with a spirit the way Jacob did. Remember that until Jacob wrestled with his angel his name was not changed to

Israel. Change of name can only come when you wrestle. **Separation is key to interaction.** You must find time to pray alone despite your busy schedule. If you are busy during the day, you can maximize the night. This is the reason why some people go to the mountain to pray. It is not because there is something special about a mountain or that spirit dwells there, it is so that they may have the time to be alone without distraction.

Proverb 18:1

Through desire a man, having separated himself, seeketh and intermeddleth with all wisdom. KJV

The undoing of many believers in interacting with spirits to gain access to hidden wisdom or breakthrough is because they spend more time with people than with God. You should take a time out and be left alone. If you are working for an organization or government, take a vacation and travel out. You can book yourself into a hotel for some days and spend time alone and you will be happy you did. You should take your bible and some books relating to the challenge or need and go on the journey and by the time you returned, everyone will know that you met with God.

Jacob knew that if he stays with his family the change he needed will not come and so he separated himself from them and came back with a new name. If you are self-employed or have a business that you can decide to leave at will, take a time out and when you are back, that business will take a new turn. It was when Moses turned aside that God spoke to him through the burning bush, Exodus 3:3-4. **When you turn aside from others to focus on God, He will surely speak to you.** Do not spend a whole year without finding time to separate yourself from people to meet with God. If you cannot stay without your family or friends, why should you stay away from God all through the year?

Spending time on the family altar of prayer and going to church is not enough, you must try and spend time alone with God. If you don't have time to travel to a mountain or book yourself into a hotel, you can wake up at night and go to a quiet place where you can wrestle with your angel alone. God may have sent an angel to bring your package but every time he wants to deliver you are surrounded by people. Maybe there is a special message attached to your package and he must deliver it to you alone.

Create a time when you can be alone with God so that He can reveal to you that which you must do or the next phase of your life. It was when I go out to meet with God alone when life was difficult that He told me what to do and when I did it, my life took a total turnaround. If I had kept being surrounded by people, you may not read this book. Writing this book is an example of being left alone. You cannot write this or receive inspiration if you don't separate yourself. Your angel can only wrestle with you when you are left alone. Jacob did not orchestrate the wrestling; he only saw himself wrestling with a man he knew was not human.

When you create the atmosphere for the spirit to interact with you, they will come without you programming them. The occultist knows the mystery of being left alone that is why they have special rooms in their house where no one is allowed to enter. This special or secret room is where they interact with demonic beings and when they come out, things begin to happen for them.

When I was a young boy, my stepdad used to lock himself inside our sitting room at midnight and would not open it to anyone. One night my mom forced the door open because she heard people talking inside and knew that we did not have visitors. When she opened the door, a mysterious wind blew and carried things inside the house. If my mom was not born again and filled with the Spirit of God, I believe she would have died that night. What my stepfather was doing at the time is what I call interacting with spirits. He separated himself from his family so that he can wrestle with spirits.

A born-again child of God who cannot separate himself or herself may never have a spiritual experience that will distinguish him or her in life. If you want to collect things from the spiritual realm, you must learn to separate yourself. If you want a spirit to visit you, you must separate yourself. Most of the inventions and discoveries did not happen when men spend time with people. They often live lonely life just to bring things into reality.

When I started this journey with God after I lost my mom and no one was around to guide me, I would separate myself from my friends and roommates a few minutes before midnight and go to an uncompleted church building to pray. Thank God I was able to do that. The people I separated myself from were evangelists and pastors and were very prominent in their church. At the time I left them to go and pray alone, they were on Facebook and midnight calls. I was a nobody. Today, the difference is clear. The pastor and evangelist who spent time on social media and midnight calls are far below where I am now. I separated myself to be left alone and wrestled with my angel and my story has changed.

If you will separate yourself from people and be left alone, you will wrestle with your angel and your life will certainly not be the same. If you truly love your family and want the best for them, leave them so that you can wrestle with your angel and when you are back, their life will become better. If Jacob did not take the opportunity of separating himself from his family that night, he would have missed it, and maybe he would not have survived the next day. Let circumstance and situations push you to a place where you can spend time alone with God. No matter how busy life might be, seek a place where you can always spend time alone with God and you will soon wrestle with the angel that is carrying your blessing and change of name.

May God grant you the grace to take responsibility and separate yourself so that you can wrestle with your angel and collect what God has for you.

Chapter 32

The Spirit of Grace and Supplication

Zechariah 12:10

And I will pour upon the house of David, and upon the inhabitants of Jerusalem, **the spirit of grace and of supplications**: *and they shall look upon me whom they have pierced, and they shall mourn for him, as one mourneth for his only son, and shall be in bitterness for him, as one that is in bitterness for his firstborn.* KJV

So far, we have learned how to cook prayer and we have explored protocols and methods that can help us cook answer delivering prayer. However, it is important to know that to pray effectively, we must be baptized with the spirit of grace and supplication. Without the spirit of grace and supplication, it will be difficult to pray. Prayer is hard work as we have learned and only the spirit of grace and supplication can help us on the altar of prayer. Without this spirit, no one will be able to pray as they ought to or cook the right prayer.

The reason why God pours upon His children the spirit of grace and supplication is so that they may be able to offer the right prayer and be enabled on the altar of prayer. For you to be effective in the kingdom of God, you must be baptized with a spirit and each baptism is for a specific assignment. When God wants to empower you to do anything for Him, He gives you a spirit. Ability in the kingdom of God is a result of the spirit at work.

Understand that everything in the kingdom of God is done by a spirit and the spirit is personality.

If you want wisdom, God will not blow air to you or drop something in you that makes you wise, He will give you the spirit of wisdom. He will cause a person of wisdom to possess you and you will begin to express the personality of that spirit.

The spirit of grace and supplication is a personality, and when you are possessed with this personality you begin to express his character. What people will see is that you can pray, and your prayer produces results but what they don't understand is that you are expressing the character of a personality. One of the spirits a born-again Christian should crave is the spirit of grace and supplication. This is the spirit that will make you a highflyer on the earth. If you can pray, anything can happen. Remember we said that there is no powerful man of God but a prayerful man of God, and when you pray both heaven and hell respond.

To cook the right prayer, you need the spirit of grace and supplication. No matter the ingredients that you gather to cook your prayer, without the spirit of grace and supplication that prayer food is bound to spoil. It is the spirit of grace that helps you through the cooking process if not, halfway to the cooking you might switch off the stove and end the cooking.

Prayer will become a burden if there is no spirit of grace and supplication. The reason why Jesus prayed through, was that he had the spirit of grace and supplication. Remember Jesus was given the spirit without measure, John 3:34. The spirit of grace and supplication helped Jesus to succeed in his earthly ministry. All through the gospel, we know that Jesus was always praying, and prayer is the only way we can generate power to succeed in our assignment. Effective prayer life can only be powered by the spirit of grace and supplication at work in any yielded vessel.

If you want to pray effectively, ask God for a fresh baptism of the spirit of grace and supplication. If you want to succeed as a Christian, you need the baptism of this spirit. I will say that if you want anything valuable in the kingdom, you should seek first the baptism of the spirit of grace and supplication and you will have anything you want in life.

Everything God has for us as His children hang on prayer and only prayer can empower us to fulfill our destiny. When you are empowered to pray, everything in life becomes a workover. Wisdom and faith as good as they are, requires prayer to function, and can only be sustained by prayer.

The kingdom of darkness fears a believer who prays more than a wise believer. Prayer is what can procure anything for us in this life thus making the spirit of grace and supplication the most important possession in the kingdom.

As you crave for this spirit and go after it with all your might, God shall baptize you afresh and your prayer altar will burn with fire. As a priest, you will stand and legislate the matters of the kingdom routing the gates of hell out of your territory in Jesus' name. I pray that you are baptized afresh with the spirit of grace and supplication so that you become a terror to the kingdom of darkness and the plan and purposes of God shall be fulfilled in your life in Jesus' name.

Epilogue

Ephesians 6:10
Finally, my brethren, be strong in the Lord, and in the power of his might. KJV

It has been a wonderful journey of learning what it takes to cook prayer that produces an answer. Now the choice is yours and the power is in your hand. You now know what it takes to live an overcomer's life and how you can enjoy all the blessings of God in your life with joy and peace. I believe from this moment going forward, you will enjoy prayer. Prayer will no longer be a burden but an interesting engagement. I sincerely believe that your Christian journey will be fruitful, and no devil will be able to confront or stand before you because of what you have learned from this book.

Prayer is hard work and not an easy task. It takes a lot to pray. In prayer, you exert both physical and spiritual energy, therefore, you must be strong. The scripture above says be strong in the Lord. You should draw strengths from God to be able to stand strong on the altar of prayer. Do not take prayer to be a casual engagement because physical strength is not what is needed to cook prayer.

Know that we are living in the last days and demonic activities will continue to be on the increase; this is to prepare the way for the antichrist. The world will experience lawlessness and wickedness will be on the increase. The only way to stay in the faith is the knowledge of how to cook prayer. As a child of God, you should never lose guard but be alert and prepared to confront every assault from the camp of the enemy.

The only thing that can keep you going in your Christian walk is prayer and the knowledge of how to pray will help you to stand out and stand well.

There will be temptations from all sides as the devil and his agents will launch all manner of attacks but when you are armed with a well-cooked prayer, you will prevail.

From this book, you have learned that prayer is a deliberate act and not a spontaneous engagement. If you keep entering the prayer room without first preparing your mind and putting things together, especially scriptures, you will come out frustrated.

From now on, before you pray, go to them that sell and gather prayer ingredients relevant to the kind of prayer food you want to cook. The best and only market that I know you can buy your prayer ingredients is the Bible, and you don't need money to make any purchase,

Isaiah 55:1

Ho, every one that thirsteth, come ye to the waters, and he that hath no money; come ye, buy, and eat; yea, come, buy wine and milk without money and without price.

HOW TO COOK PRAYER

The Bible is God's market, and you can buy anything you want without a price tag. Go to that market and purchase whatever you want, and it will be given to you. Do not allow anyone to deceive you that you must be a great man of God before you can overcome every unwanted challenge in your life.

In the Bible, you can purchase children, a husband, a successful business, career elevation, a peaceful home, and financial prosperity, including peace, and joy, among other ingredients. All these are sold in the Bible market, and you can take them to prepare a nice prayer meal that others will enjoy eating with you.

As a man, remember that you are the priest of your family, and the peace and prosperity of your home depend on you. It is time you live a higher spiritual life through an effective prayer life. As a wife, cook your husband and children on the prayer altar and they will live healthy and fulfilled. As a minister, you have no other source of power for your ministry except prayer. As a businessperson, the power to get wealth can only come through prayer.

As a politician, do not play politics with an empty eye else you will not go far. Your colleagues are very diabolical and the only way to stand against them is through an effective prayer life.

Whoever you are, the only way you can live well on this earth and break through each stage of your life is by prayer. Your last prayer can only go as far if you don't keep the fire on your prayer altar burning.

Now that you have been equipped with this knowledge, make prayer your addiction. We are entering into a time of great distress and the only thing that will keep us going is prayer. When you make prayer your faithful companion, you will dominate. Everything around you will be secured; you will be kept intact and ready for the master's return.

Ephesians 3:16

That he would grant you, according to the riches of his glory, to be strengthened with might by his Spirit in the inner man. KJV

I pray that God Strengthens you with might in your spirit to stand strong on the altar of prayer. We are entering a season of great distress; the Bible calls it the *distress of nations*. New diseases will come up, and crime will be on the increase. COVID 19 was a test run, the worst will keep coming. It takes prayer to stay above the trial.

A time is coming when many believers will deny the faith and leave the church according to 2 Thessalonians 2:3. It will be a perilous time 2 Timothy 3:1. You can overcome and make it to the mark if you give yourself to prayer. The devil has entered the heart of many people to carry out wickedness in these last days, but when you pray, you will overcome.

I pray that the knowledge you get from this book will keep you in faith through a committed prayer life. We may never meet here on earth, but I will see you in glory when the trumpet sound. God Bless You.

JESUS THE SAME YESTERDAY, TODAY AND FOR EVER

If you have been blessed, impacted, or given your life to Jesus through reading this book, please reach out through the following:

Email: victoransor@yahoo.com

website: victoransor.com

GOD BLESS YOU

www.ingramcontent.com/pod-product-compliance
Lightning Source LLC
Chambersburg PA
CBHW060349080526
44583CB00012B/237